the cost of
dis**obedience**

what price will you pay

by Felecia Portwood

S.H.E. PUBLISHING, LLC

The Cost of Disobedience | What Price Will You Pay?
Copyright © 2022 by Felecia Portwood.

All rights reserved. Printed in the United States of America. No part of this book may be used or reproduced in any manner whatsoever without written permission except in the case of brief quotations embodied in critical articles or reviews.

For information contact: **www.shepublishingllc.com** or
info@shepublsihingllc.com

Cover and Title Page Design by Michelle Phillips of

CHELLD3 3D VISUALIZATION AND DESIGN

ISBN: 978-1-953163-51-6

First Edition: November 2022

10 9 8 7 6 5 4 3 2 1

CONTENTS

INTRODUCTION	I
THE DAWN | CHAPTER 1	1
THE TWILIGHT | CHAPTER 2	11
THE DUSK | CHAPTER 3	19
THE PREY | CHAPTER 4	30
THE WARNING | CHAPTER 5	42
THE FOUNDATION | CHAPTER 6	53
THE BREACH | CHAPTER 7	64
THE SEPARATION | CHPATER 8	73
THE DESCENT | CHAPTER 9	87

THE FALL | CHAPTER 10	95
THE RELEASE | CHAPTER 11	119
ABOUT THE AUTHOR	131

INTRODUCTION

I remember it like it was yesterday, so long ago. Sitting next to my husband as we were driving home, I was wracked with sadness and my heart was heavy. My life was falling apart right before my eyes. Every day, every hour, every minute, disruption seemed all-consuming and all around me. Even when I thought things were coming together, something else would revolt against me.

I began to speak to God in silence. "God, what have I done so wrong? Why am I going through so much hell?"

I can't explain exactly what happened next, except to say a small, still voice whispered, "Write the book." I looked over at my husband, but I knew it wasn't him. He was fixated on the road ahead. Something stirred deep inside of me when I heard these four words that changed my life forever: "The Cost of Disobedience".

When I was growing up, if any child in our house (sister, brother, cousin, or friend) disobeyed a rule or instruction, we would be chastised. Whether we had something we liked taken away or whether we got our backsides spanked, we had a price to pay. In that same way, God chastises His children. When we do contrary to what He tells us to do, there will be a chastising.

Proverb 3:12
For the LORD corrects those He loves, just as a father corrects a child in whom he delights.

1 Samuel 15:22
To obey is better than sacrifice, and to hearken more than the fat of rams.

I pray that what you read blesses you as God has blessed me, and I encourage you to obey what you read of the LORD's words concerning you.

THE DAWN

Chapter 1

I HAD BEEN LIVING AN ADULT LIFESTYLE SINCE I WAS 16 years old, when I gave birth to my first child. At 29 years old, I felt quite wise and knowledgeable when it came to love and relationships. Thirteen years and four kids later... Wow! Was I wrong!

In 2004, I was one (1) year divorced from my first husband, raising four (4) beautiful children, and in a new relationship that seemed promising. I worked full time during the day and enjoyed coming home to take care of my family. While nursing as an LPN is my profession, I also enjoy taking care of and helping people any way I can. Giving love and kindness comes easy for me.

While it may take months or years for some to recover from divorce, the moment I walked out that door, my life never skipped a beat. My attitude was simple: "I am fine, and life goes on!" It also helped that I met this guy while going through my divorce, and he made the transition seem less stressful. He was God-fearing, family-oriented, and handsome as a prince. I think it's safe to say he was "Ginuwine Fine." If you were to ask him what his strongest quality is, he would probably say, "I am a perfect gentleman." Yes, that was one of his strongest qualities.

From the moment we met, we enjoyed each other's company, conversations, and visions for the future. We had something special and after six months of dating, we moved in together. Too soon? Some would probably say yes, but as an adult woman with four children, a thriving career, and an internal drive to move forward from a failed marriage, I thought it would be okay. I was restored enough to move forward. So, we moved into a spacious three-bedroom apartment: my kids, my new boo and I. I loved this place at first sight, mostly because as a child, I lived in that very same complex, and had a lot of good memories that have stayed with me to this day. Another reason I loved the apartment is because it just felt like home from the moment, I viewed it and applied for residency.

With two daughters and two sons, the apartment was a perfect fit. Having three bedrooms, my girls shared a bedroom, my boys shared a bedroom and then there was my bedroom. This was truly a place anyone would call home. My companion at that time, who I will refer to as Peter, had two daughters and they would come over to stay on weekends and during school breaks and they would pool in the room with my girls. The girls were beautiful and yes, they were daddy's little girls: spoiled, but respectful always. All the children were spoiled to a certain degree, but his girls could get away with things my children could not. I was sterner with rules and when it came to discipline, my children knew what was not allowed or tolerated. However, at the end of the day, it worked itself out. Peter loved his girls and was big on family values and he would let it be known at every opportunity.

One of the most fulfilling aspects of this relationship was the love of his family. Every woman desires a mother-in-law who adores and respects her, no matter what and a sister-in-law who seems like she was cut from the same cloth as you. When you can connect and love your mate's siblings as your own, it doesn't get any better than that. I'm talking about true, genuine, and loyal people who know your flaws and still love you no matter what. It is true, 'what's from the heart reaches the heart'. This family knows how to give and receive love. I don't see that these days among families and siblings. What I usually see is backbiting, selfishness, disloyalty, and disrespect on all levels among friends, in-laws, family and even extended families. It appears morals have drifted away in the wind.

Often, we would host family gatherings at our place. Occasionally, I would prepare large meals and invite both our families over and sometimes I would just do simple things like have coffee and play board games with our family. Dominoes always ruled. We always resorted to dominoes before the night was over. We would spend hours together, sometimes until the wee hours of the morning, eating, laughing, and watching Peter get on his mother's nerves. It was priceless! It wasn't that getting on her nerves was funny; it was the behavior and actions he would carry out that were hilarious. Not to mention the nieces and nephews that just kept my stomach aching from laughing so hard. Laughter is truly good for the soul.

There wasn't a day that went by where we didn't either see or speak to Peter's family. There was never a time that I felt like I saw too much of them. Let's be honest, we all have someone in our family who we wouldn't mind if we didn't see them so often. Am I right? This family, however, did not fit into that category. Peter and I lived only blocks away from some of my immediate family, so we would drive by daily or almost daily to say hello and see if my grandmother needed anything. Time spent with my family was minimal compared to Peter's family. My family is not as large as his, and we were all we had. My siblings and I love each other; however, we all have commitments that keep us busy and get in the way of family time. Although my family would come to the gatherings I hosted, at that time we didn't share the bond that Peter's family displayed every day. I am grateful that lately I have spent some very meaningful time with my sisters and brothers. It's been a long time coming and I look forward to the days ahead.

It is my belief that there are several important factors in the making and bonding of family and relationships. One of those factors is building a foundation in Christ and being connected with a man or woman of God who holds a place of leadership. There are many things to be learned in the church that we just may not fully acknowledge, accept or simply understand about life and how to cope. Things such as true forgiveness and how to love unconditionally. This is a quality that Peter's family displayed to all who were connected to them.

While Peter and his family stole my heart from the start, there was another very significant person who changed my life forever. When we began dating, Peter invited me to a celebration for his pastor. Peter was God-fearing and if at all humanly possible, would fight Lucifer face-to-face to save his pastor. One night, I can't remember if it was the church's anniversary or the pastor's birthday extravaganza, but Peter's entire family was attending the celebration. At the time, going to church was an occasional thing for me. As a matter of fact, I can't recall how long it had been prior to attending with Peter. Needless to say, I accepted the invitation to what I thought was a kind gesture, only to have my heart stolen by yet another woman connected to Peter's family.

Once we arrived at the celebration, Peter introduced me to many people in his life. Once he made his appearance felt across the room, we were seated. Everyone knew Peter and if by chance someone didn't, they would have known him by the end of the night. While I felt a little out of place at first, I found that being in the presence of "church folks" made me feel welcomed. Everyone was happy and smiling. It was a jovial event. People were greeting me and loving on me as if they knew me for years.

As the festivities began, joy blanketed the room. Some people gave speeches and others sang songs of worship. We ate and then everyone sang more songs! Just as the night was coming to an end, this beautiful, gentle woman with a smile that was guaranteed to melt your soul, came over to the table where we were seated and quietly asked me a question. "Did you enjoy yourself?" I replied, "Yes ma'am, I did." This beautiful, soft spoken woman was Peter's Pastor. Apostle Flo Jo ! She then invited me to attend the church whenever I had time. She was warm, friendly, and genuine.

Church was like second nature for this family. It wasn't long before I started attending regularly with Peter; and I must admit, it was very fulfilling. Until then, I never attended a storefront church or any church that packed the kind of power that reigned in that place. When the choir sang, it seemed like the angels were sitting in our very presence. Moreover, when the pastor brought forth the Word for the hour, it seemed as if Jesus himself was speaking directly to us.

Whenever the pastor would preach, the house would be full. Apostle oversees a few churches in different locations, so that requires her to be away at times. I think I can safely say that the church as a whole did not like it when the pastor was away. Not because no one else was qualified, it was just that we wanted the true raw Word in a context that only our pastor could deliver. Although she is gentle and always smiling when speaking to people, she would preach with such authority and clarity that nothing could ever be questioned in the realm of her assignment.

I have so much respect for this woman of God, as if she were my own mother. With all the love that flowed from her and her desire for all people to have a right relationship with God, it didn't take long for me to join the congregation. There was a new desire that took hold of me. I wanted to learn more about Christ and living right for HIS namesake. I wanted to be a better me. So, I didn't waste time. I joined EODM.

Taking those life-changing steps to the altar for redemption seemed like the longest walk ever. Although the church isn't that big, it felt like millions of people were watching me. I thought, *Okay, it's only one walk, do it and get it over with.* I stood face-to-face with the pastor as she assisted me through the Prayer of Salvation, hands lifted, tears flowing and more nervous than I had ever been about anything in my entire life. After we prayed, she hugged me and said, "God loves you and I love you, and ain't nothing you can do about it!" From that moment to this one, I love this woman with all my heart.

Sunday after Sunday, I sat in that church to hear and learn something new about how to live right and get to heaven. Even more than that, it was a family activity to attend Sunday service, then visit other family members who lived close by the church, followed by a coffee stop on the way home. While it may not sound like much to some, these little things meant the most to me. Some people only appreciate the finer things in life, like vacation trips, spending money and fancy cars, but this family made the best with less. I consider this family as a true model of what a family should be.

Occasionally, we would drive to Mississippi to fellowship with one of the other branches of the Evangelistic Outreach Deliverance Ministry (EODM) and visit friends who moved there from Chicago. The ride to Mississippi was long, but fun and memorable. Peter would drive each time, while the rest of us would laugh ourselves tired and then fall asleep on him, only to awaken if we felt a shift or swerve on the road. While we would be out of town for fellowship, it was like a vacation for all of us because we were away from home and being guests in a different environment. Every trip to Mississippi was relaxing and pleasant; even the church was filled with love and laughter. It amazed me that even the church members there carried the same humble, happy spirit as the pastor. I guess that is the way it should be if you're being led properly and live as the Bible instructs.

1 John 4:7

Beloved, let us love one another, for love is of God; and everyone who loves is born of God and knows God.

THE TWILIGHT

Chapter 2

LIFE FOR PETER AND ME SEEMED TO BE GOING GREAT. We had been dating for two years, and I wouldn't say it was perfect, but it seemed very promising to me. There was more good than bad. As with any couple, we had minor disputes and roadblocks, but no matter what the situation was, we held each other down and had each other's back. While we were not attached at the hip, we spent a lot of our time together and enjoyed the family lifestyle with our children and family to the best of our ability.

I'm not exactly sure if it's a woman's instincts or just an attribute that was passed down from my mother and grandmother, but I tend to want my man to feel like a king. I enjoy cooking for him, meeting his needs (mentally, physically, emotionally... and... um, yeah... let's keep it real... sexually) and maintaining a welcoming home environment. At this time, I had not yet understood the importance of spiritual necessity, which also nourishes a man. Again, I THOUGHT I knew it all and I gave all I had in me. While the children were always taken care of, hands down, I have always taken great pleasure in keeping my man smiling. I look for ways to make things easier or less stressful for him. I like to run the bath water while he's on his way home from work, position the slippers at the front door or at the foot of the bed, cook dinner or have it done when he walks through the door and if possible, complete any tasks that may be on our to-do list for the day, if it's doable.

I've been told that I spoil men and I do too much, but somehow, these things just come natural to me. On many occasions, my best friend, Lasagne, would ask me the same question. "Girl, what are you doing to these men?" I just laugh and say, "Nothing." She always joked about how the men I was involved with would always want me to be around them and them only. Now I am not saying that I am THE perfect woman, but I can say this: I have yet to be replaced. Imma just leave that right there.

From the very beginning, our new extended family was adjusting well, inside and outside the home. From playing Xbox with the boys to becoming the girls' basketball coach at their elementary school, Peter found his place with the kids, and it has never left them. To this day, all my children maintain a special relationship with him.

A typical day for us was me going off to work by 8:00 a.m. while Peter would be home to see the kids off to school, then he would leave the house to go to work. The children's school was a five-minute walk directly across an open field. We could literally watch them walk to school from our front window. To watch the children through the window would bring back memories for me, because this was the same elementary school my oldest brother, my first-born daughter and I attended and graduated from. Sometimes I would stand there and think of old classmates and wonder, *where are they now?*

At some point during the day one of us would call the other to see how our day was going. We would vent if we needed to or just be the other's listening ear. On occasion, Peter would surprise me by stopping by to bring me lunch while I was working. It was a kind gesture, and I was very tickled by the attention the other ladies on the unit displayed when this attractive young man gently and eloquently walked in, requesting to see me. They would all huddle up while whispering, "He fine, Girl. Wish somebody was bringing me lunch." I would just laugh it off and keep it moving, in a bashful kind of way.

Love is such a beautiful thing when two individuals share the same feelings and strive for the same goals. Love will have you rushing home from work just to be in the presence of that special someone for no other reason other than to be there. Love doesn't find fault; it finds ways to correct the wrong and reciprocate forgiveness. To love and be loved is the greatest gift of all.

There was almost never a dull moment in our day-to-day lives. We hung out as a couple, socialized in groups, and shared hobbies that were simple yet adventurous, with no regard for the time of year or season.

However, with all the time spent, moments shared, and loyalty invested, something went wrong.

After twenty-four months of love and happiness, things started turning sour. We both took on new job opportunities at the same company; something I now know was not such a good idea. Not saying that it cannot work and be successful, but both individuals must possess honest maturity and a solid commitment. It started off well and exciting until accusations of infidelity surfaced. I knew Peter was a woman-magnet because he was a very attractive man. But really? Allegations of him flirting while on the job? I was furious.

So, after long hours of work and a steady stream of rumors, instead of coming home enjoying each other, we were arguing about what was being discussed and whispered around the office. Peter would deny all of it, and I wouldn't believe a word he said. Some of the things that were being said had some believability, and if you're into your man and pay him enough attention like I did, you know he is capable of getting caught up in all the adulation.

Initially, when there were nightclub functions or invitations, we would go as a couple, but as time passed, Peter started going out alone, calling them the "Fella's night out". While it is absolutely fine for him to go out with his friends, as it turned out, every outing became a fella's night out. They were also occurring more frequently, while our outings as a couple became few and far between. Now, if there is one thing that I am, it's that I am observant. I paid attention to Peter's routines and his change in circle of friends. Before long, there were more women aboard these 'fellas' night outs. Now, when you are in a committed relationship, you must be conscious and considerate of who and what you entertain. My trust in Peter began to fade.

As the time away from home became more frequent, so did

the longer nights. He went from coming home at a decent hour to stepping in at four or five in the morning. Then there would be the early morning "private" calls that would show up on his phone. And before long, whispered calls made in the other room began to take place. Then he started leaving early for work almost every day. Even though Peter and I worked for the same company, we worked different hours. I worked in the field going into client's home, whereas: Peter spent more time in the office than I because of meetings he had to attend. Therefore, we drove separate cars.

It amazes me when men don't realize that a woman can recognize from the tone of their voice whether they are talking to a man or woman (that is to say, friend or side piece) on the phone. Then the unthinkable started to happen. I would call Peter's phone and he wouldn't answer. When I would address the issues as they came up, he would always deny them.

As sad as it was, I would do the whole "checking the phone" thing, call numbers back and track dates and times of calls, until finally, on one occasion, I had a face-to-face confrontation with him. I knew it was time, as I had lost all trust in Peter; I knew that my intelligence was being played upon. I felt insulted. During this time, I couldn't understand why Peter was exhibiting such behaviors. Being a God-fearing man, family oriented and who love and respect all the women in his life, what has caused him to switch up on me? Was I fascinated with the representation of him for these past two years, and now the real Peter is showing up or is the devil tapping on his shoulder? Either way, I'm not for NONE!

It has been said that the most loyal women are the ones who get hurt the most. This I find to be true. One would think, with all I do to establish and maintain a happy and healthy relationship, getting hurt wouldn't be on my radar anywhere. What man would mess that up? Personally, I believe if a man is not ready and mature, and readiness comes from maturity, you could be most devoted and most attentive, and he may still hurt you. In my case, Peter was acting like a man with the mind of a child.

For six months, we argued over the same stuff, but nothing changed. It came to a point where every now and then, I locked him out and he was forced to stay at his sister's place. I finally decided that I no longer wanted to be in this relationship. Once I felt that he used up the last bit of trust in my heart, everything about Peter became unattractive. Therein stood that thin line between love and hate. Although I could never really hate a person, I hated his actions and I refused to play the fool and participate in his childish games.

Romans 12:9

Don't just pretend to love others. Really love them.

Hate what is wrong. Hold tightly to what is good.

3 THE DUSK

Chapter 3

IT WAS JUNE 2006 WHEN I DECIDED THAT ENOUGH WAS enough. No more wondering what Peter was doing, no more him coming home in the wee hours of the night, and absolutely no more having to hear about his little rendezvous with our co-workers. So, this day, I carried on with my regular workday. However, my mind would not shut down. I finally came to the decision that I was going to let Peter know we were over, and he needed to move out.

When I got home that evening, Peter was relaxing on the couch in the living room watching television. I walked over to him and said in a kind voice, "Call your sister and see if you can stay there because you need to leave here." He looked confused. "What?" It was hard to believe that he was acting as if he had no idea what I was talking about.

Then he said, "Fee, you need to stop and get gone with that. I ain't going nowhere." Now, his response was not wanted, nor was it negotiable at this point. After a few minutes of going back and forth with verbal attacks, I decided to act on my instinct. More so than not, I consider myself to be loving, kind, considerate and giving. However, if I feel I have been taken advantage of or mishandled in any way, I can be stubborn, evil and a real B&%*#. When I make my mind up about a thing, I will not deviate from that. My mind was made up: I WAS DONE!

After many requests for Peter to leave to which he declined every time, he left me only one solid option. Within fifteen minutes, there were two peace officer's downstairs responding to my call. I told them that I asked Peter to leave, and he was refusing. After a brief conversation, one of the officers asked Peter to come downstairs and speak with him, so he did.

Peter went back and forth with the officer, stating his claim and why he shouldn't be made to leave his home. Luckily for me, Peter didn't exactly know his rights and eventually, with the peace officers standing by, he ended up gathering some of his belongings and left the house. In case you are wondering, individuals have rights to their residence if they have been staying there and have established a tenancy. While I am not proud of the way things ended and how I got Peter to leave, I was simply fed up with his dishonesty. I was not going to share space with him one more day. Although I never caught him in the presence of another woman, all the red flags were there, and he could never give me a concrete response to any of my questions or concerns I knew he would end up at his sister's place and that he would be okay. Although I was done, I was comfortable with knowing that he was not on the streets and had a place to go.

After Peter drove off, one of the officers walked over to me and said, "You shouldn't be dealing with drama and when you are ready, you can call me, and I will show you how to live and have fun." I laughed and said with a smile, "Thank you, but no thank you. I just want peace." The officer turned to walk away, but not before repeating his offer. I continued laughing as I walked inside. The gesture was cute, but I am thinking, *some men will try to get a catch anywhere, in any situation*. Here I am with a germy nursing uniform on, ponytail wet from the rain and in the middle of a verbal domestic situation with a shitty mood, and this man is trying to get his Mack on. Really?

A few days passed and while I was still communicating with

Peter's family I certainly didn't want to talk to Peter. Regardless of the spats we had, his family and I maintained our friendship. The home front was at peace, and I was thinking I could get used to this 'single' thing. It was only a few days, so boredom or loneliness did not yet kick in. Besides, Peter wasn't too far from me because I would still see him on Sundays in church. Church was church as usual, I still sat and fellowshipped with Peter's family and our church family. Occasionally, those days were bittersweet, but I made it through and didn't wear my feelings on my sleeve. I cut back on the post church outing with the family, but I still maintain our phone communications with them and visited them on occasions.

So, one day I was on the phone with my best friend discussing the whole breakup thing and how I was keeping myself occupied and the other line rings. It wasn't a number that I recognized from the Caller ID, so I answered it with a bit of hesitation.

A man with a soft voice said, "Hello young lady, how are you?"

"I'm sorry," I said. "Who is this?"

"Officer Isharat," he replied.

Somewhat shocked, I answered, "I'm fine. How did you get my number?"

"You called for assistance the other day, didn't you?" he asked. "The number you called from showed up on the system."

"WOW!" was all I could say.

The conversation lasted a few minutes. I guess you could call it a wellness check. He asked how I was doing, and I assured him that I was okay and thanked him for his concern. At the end of the call, he said he would call again in a few days to check up on me.

He kept his word. Within a few days, he called again to check on me, and also see if I was "ready to live a little and have some fun," as he described it. Again, I thanked him for his concern and told him I wasn't sure about the fun part. I told him to call back the next day and I would let him know. That was just my way of getting off the phone with him. All in all, he was respectful and a bit charming during each call. It was "creep" behavior, but I didn't sense any negative vibes.

This went on for a couple of weeks, and I purposely ignored his calls at times. That is, until that one hot summer day when I had nothing to do, and the last thing I wanted was to sit around the house all day. When he called, I took him up on his proposal and agreed to go out for a date later that evening. It had only been a few weeks since Peter and I broke up and I took this as an opportunity to just get out the house for the evening.

Judas came by my place to pick me up and we spent the evening dining out and having simple conversations. It wasn't a long night, but it was pleasant and fulfilling for the most part. After hours of laughter, he got me back safely to my place. As he pulled up to the curb, I told him I enjoyed myself and I thanked him for the fun time we had. He said I was most welcome and asked if he could see me again. I was coy about it and told him to give me a call in a few days. I could have just said yes or no then, but why not indulge in the chase?

Within a couple of weeks, Judas and I shared a second night out. With no planned agenda, we ultimately ended up at his female cousin's house. It was her birthday, so we stepped out with her and another cousin for a night of celebration. We talked, we laughed, we drank cocktails, and we danced the night away.

Judas was consistently charming throughout the night. He complimented me often and went above and beyond to ensure that I was having a good time. After four hours of celebrating his cousin's birthday we were exhausted and elated. What a wonderful time! It feels good when I meet people for the first time, and we click so well that having a good time comes easy! What a night!

As the evening came to an end, Judas' cousin thanked me for coming out, then turned to Judas and said, "I like her, she's not stuck up, she's fun and down to earth." Judas reached for my hand and said, "I like her, too."

Tickled and tipsy, I advanced toward the exit and Judas followed. Being on top of his game, Judas opened the doors and covered me with his blazer jacket to keep me warm. He was smooth and cute in a caring way. He was surely representing himself well on this date.

Judas got me home in thirty minutes, safe and sound again. We thanked each other for a wonderful night. I could tell he enjoyed our date. He walked me to the front entrance of my apartment complex, and as we stood at the gate, he kissed me softly on my cheek and said he would call me the next day.

"Sure. That sounds great," I said with a smile. Once in the gate and through the main entrance, Judas pulled away slowly down the street, watching me until I was out of his view and inside the hallway area.

The night was fun, but boy was I worn out. Generally, the first few dates with anyone new are always stressful for me. I love to sip on cocktails and dance away the night, but all I ever want to do after a night like that is get in my bed and sleep for the next twelve hours.

Sharing long phone calls with Judas became a regular thing, and after several more dates and meaningful conversations, we both began to realize that we had something special. He was aware of my relationship status and hardly ever talked about his, although once he mentioned that he was in the process of settling his divorce. He was living at his parents' house, in their basement. Judas has a gift when it comes to building and he renovated and reconstructed his living quarters to mimic a one-bedroom apartment, lacking nothing. He said that because he works so much, he's hardly ever home and only sleeping there during his off hours of work.

One of my biggest problems is that I tend not to pry too much into a man's personal business or ask a lot of questions soon enough, I suppose. I will take a person's word for what he or she says, until things start looking shady or not add up. That being said, I would say that I learned from our conversations that he was not currently in a relationship and was looking forward to his divorce being finalized he never gave me details as to why he was getting a divorce. He only mentioned that his family didn't care for his wife and that his wife was not a good mother because she never kept her son at home with them. He said the son was always at the grandmother's house. She too was a peace officer and he never spoke about her during conversations. With no motive intended, I encouraged Judas to do what's best for him and not let a bad situation get the best of him.

I encouraged him to live every day to the fullest, and not be stressed out about life and living. Recently divorced myself, I knew that divorce can be a battle and it takes a sound and calm mind to not be overcome and feel defeated or that you were a failure. Deal with the new parameters.

Judas was honest with me when he said that he was going through his second divorce. He said his first wife lived downstate, and they shared three children together. At the time, the children were adolescents and into young adulthood. Judas said that he and his children's mother have a very good co-parenting relationship, as well as friendship. I was glad to hear that he was active in his children's lives, because so many fathers become extinct after they split from their wives. Fathers hold a very important role in their children's lives. Unfortunately, so many women cheat their children out of what's needed for them to grow up emotionally healthy because of their own selfish reasons. Often, it is the anger that women hold for the father that makes her use the children as pawns in an already broken relationship.

Children need both parents in their lives; otherwise, there will always be a void, whether the child is a boy or a girl. This child will become aware of what is missing and the way they now live. A mother's decision to hold back her kids from their father will no doubt have a negative emotional impact on the kids for years to come.

I have known plenty of men who took the back seat in their

children's lives because they were no longer married to the children's mom; yet they take care of stepchildren with no problem. It's sad that children always get caught up in the mess of selfish and immature adults. It's our job as parents to raise our children to the best of our ability, whether we remain a couple or not. Thank GOD this was not Judas' story, based on what he told me. Judas didn't speak too much about his second wife, only that the family was divided.

Psalm 127:3

Behold, children are a heritage from the LORD,

the fruit of the womb is a reward.

THE PREY

Chapter 4

JUDAS AND I DEVELOPED A PATTERN OF WHEN WE WOULD get together and hangout based upon our individual schedules. With about two months into our relationship, we were still hanging tight and his visits to my place became more frequent. Basically, we were just enjoying each other's company learning about our journeys and having fun.

I was intentional in not having him around my children

immediately because we were not there yet. Ours was just fun. It worked out well because he was usually over when my kids were at my grandparents' place, a couple of blocks away. They liked going there because that's where their friends hung out. Also, because they knew that anything goes at Grandma's house, so they enjoyed being out of our house. It was too soon to introduce Judas to them. The children still had Peter in their system, and they were being low key about hoping for his return. More than that, Judas and I were not an item, so it wasn't an issue.

With Judas working the graveyard shift, he would come by the house during his down time or when activity was at a minimum. We would lay across the chaise lounge together in the living room, talking and watching movies until we fell asleep, or he got a call over his radio. Some nights he wouldn't get a call at all, and we would just be in chill mode.

If we weren't lounging on the couch, he would be patrolling his beat, talking on the phone all night long with me. Things between us were cool. I was enjoying his company. He was fun to look at – everything was in place: his uniform, his style when he wasn't in uniform, and I was delighted to find out that his ability to smell so good from the colognes he wore was outstanding! There's nothing like a man who smells good all the time. I guess I should mention here, there was just one thing that was not so attractive (to me) about Judas. He had that nicotine urge to light up a cigarette more often than not. Otherwise, he had it going on. At the time, I thought smoking was what he did to relieve the stress that cops go through on any given night.

While we were still early in the game and we were just having fun, I was kind of liking the attention and company. Before long, we turned things up a notch. He was coming by every day, and we were both happy to see each other. When his shift was done, he would come over and I would cook him a great meal, then he would sleep for a few hours before going home to finish working on his mom's basement.

Mornings with Judas were, in a word, outstanding. I don't know if it was me, the food, the job or maybe the combination of it all that would have him sleeping like a baby. I would like to think it was my way of taking care of someone who is important to me. Now, after a full night of sleep, my energy level is always way, way up and what better way to start the day than with some huggin' and lovin' with that man waking up right next to me... if you catch my drift.

The day started like every other Tuesday, until the evening rolled around. To set the record straight, it is a day I will never forget. Judas and I established a routine that worked for us; but there came a time when I felt that our familiar habits and actions were repetitious, bordering on boring.

Let me explain. After an uneventful day at work, then some quality time spent with the kids, then cleaning and straightening up the house, and ending the day running errands, I knew what was next. Judas would start his shift at work and if things weren't too busy, he would possibly get a chance to come over. Keeping my hopes up with great anticipation, I would search for a movie that we could watch together. I would make sure there was a cold Pepsi and popcorn waiting for us to cozy up on the yellow chaise lounge. As usual, the night was quiet, and work was minimal. Judas arrived at my place; we made ourselves comfortable and started watching a movie until the movie watched us. Rarely would we ever get through a full movie without falling asleep, but to be honest, falling asleep together was the best part.

Around two o'clock in the morning, the ringing from his phone woke me up. Judas didn't budge, and when it rang again for the third time, I figured it was an emergency, so I woke him up. He checked the caller ID and dialed the number back. After he said, "Hello," with such urgency, he said, "I'm on my way."

Judas jumped up from the chaise, put his shoes on and walked toward the door. Then he stopped and turned around to come closer to me and said, "I'll call you later."

I kissed his cheek and said, "Okay." Then I locked the door behind him as I wondered about all the possibilities of that call. For some reason I cannot explain, something told me that there was either an emergency with his mom or someone was having a baby. Of all the things it could have been, this is what I sensed it was because of the tone in his voice and his swift exit.

Knowing that morning would come quick enough, I turned off the television in the living room and went to bed. As I lay there under the covers, my head swirled with worry. I hoped everything was okay.

The next day when mid-afternoon came around, I still hadn't heard from Judas. That was unusual, but given his emergency exit, I felt like I would just wait for him to call me and not disturb him. Instead, I called my BFF. Our conversations are always exciting and full of girl stuff, like what my man says or what her man does or *was it good*? Ha! Don't judge me! We've all done it.

At the time, Lasagne and I had been friends for about sixteen years. We talk about everything, and we know about everything that is going on in each other's life.

I told her about Judas having to leave on an emergency and I told her about the reasons behind my guesses. She laughed when I told her my baby theory.

"Fee, you crazy! But hey, you never know!"

The more we talked, the more I told her about Judas. Things like *as far as I knew, Judas didn't have a woman in his life*. Those were his words, and he never mentioned anything about the woman he was divorcing being pregnant. There were too many "what ifs" here, so I tried to put it aside and get on with my day. I remember hoping that all would be well. *On with my day*, I thought.

Thirty-two hours later, I finally got his call. While I was certainly glad to hear from him, I was feeling some type of way... like he put me on 'hold' until he was ready to call. I answered with a "Good morning. How are you?"

It was 10:00 a.m. and he sounded like he just woke up. He apologized for not calling me the day before and went on to say that he was very tired. I asked him if everything was okay, and to my surprise, he said, "Yes, I just had a baby girl." For a quick minute, I was at a loss for words. Sitting on the couch, my mouth dropped wide open. I said to myself, *WHAT?!*

Once my heart jumped back up from my stomach into my chest, I said, "Congratulations." He ended the call by saying, "I'm going to try and get some rest now, but I promise I will see you today; I want to see you today if it's okay with you."

"It's cool. You get some rest," I said. "Just call me later."

Well, how about that? My thoughts were right. Somebody *has* had a baby. At that point, I was tripping, but not really tripping. News like that isn't something a woman just predicts she will hear; and it is certainly not the news that she cares to hear at this point in a relationship.

I was trying to replay that conversation we had about his divorce in progress, but I couldn't for the life of me remember him saying there was a baby on the way. We were almost two months into this relationship, which included almost-daily visits. We had a few personal and intimate conversations, but none included the word, pregnancy.

Now, to me, this is relevant information. Two months into a very comfortable and loving routine with a man I was liking a little bit more every time we were together, I found the news a bitter pill to swallow. Although we were not yet official, I was digging this fine man, and now suddenly, the game changed.

Once again, I had to talk this out with Lasagne and let her know that I am not crazy. When she answered my call, I blurted out my news right away. I spilled out my feelings and thoughts and told her about my position on all of it. Finally, after that long conversation with Lasagne, who always looks out for me (and I for her), I decided that I didn't want any part of a relationship with a man who has a new baby with an ex or potential ex-wife.

Again, as far as I knew, Judas was not dating anyone outside of the two of us "hanging out," so I assumed his soon-to-be ex-wife had the baby. I know that new babies require a lot of attention, and some women use babies for pawns, attention, booty calls and every other deceitful thing they can come up with. Who knows? This birth may even be a rebuilding factor and may put the divorce on hold or even cancel it. I know it may have sounded harsh, because I, too, was a newly single parent of four children, but this was something I was not up for. I am not interested in dating a man with small children. Some Baby Mommas are too demanding, and my buttons are not the ones to push.

After waiting patiently throughout the day, Judas finally came by later that evening. He was very forthright about the new baby and what was going on. No, his soon-to-be ex-wife did not have a baby. There was another woman that he so conveniently never mentioned. Somewhere between leaving his wife and meeting me in July of 2006, he was involved with a woman named Luci. Well, Luci lived across the state line and according to Judas, she was a "hook up" through a mutual friend.

Judas said the relationship between him, and Luci was brief and that they were no longer an item. I asked why and he said that Luci was overall not his type, and she had no control over her teenage daughter, noting that the daughter talks back to Luci and that he once had to break Luci and the daughter up from fighting one another. He went on to say that he thought Luci's pregnancy was a set-up on her part to rekindle their relationship.

Judas claimed that he was under the impression that Luci was on birth control.

According to him, he and Luci had, in fact, broken up and she got pregnant while on a trip to California that the two of them had previously planned and paid for together before the breakup. He told me that Luci contacted him to say that even though they were not together, she still wanted to take the trip, so he obliged. Two months after the trip, Luci contacted him out of the blue to say that she was pregnant. Judas told me that he was clear with Luci that he didn't want any more kids; but obviously, the decision was hers to make. So, there you have it... a beautiful baby girl.

My facial expressions most times tell my thoughts before my mouth can ever speak it. After listening attentively to this elaborate story, I told Judas why I did not want to go any further with him and our relationship. I was very intentional about letting it be known that I don't do drama and I surely don't want to be a wedge between a father and his child. I went so far as to explain to him how emotional and vulnerable women get after the birth of a baby. I shed some wisdom with him by saying that a woman can make a man's life with a "New Boo" pure hell if she, in fact, was using the baby as a way back into the man's life.

Judas assured me that he and Luci had "been over" and there were no chances of them ever getting back together. He

39 | THE COST OF DISOBEDIENCE

looked me straight in the eyes and, without blinking, said he wanted to continue to see me.

With our relationship staying more consistent, with Judas assuring me that he was not involved with this woman, I wanted to feel a sense of relief. Nevertheless, going against everything I believed, I continued to see him. He already met my children, and I was happy about how that played out. Within a few days of meeting my kids, Judas showed up with his baby daughter for my children and me to meet her. We all hovered over her like she was a new toy. She was as cute as a button, and she hardly ever cried. During the time she was with us, Judas would lay her between us on the bed and watch her sleep while we were watching television. Times like these were priceless. Everything felt right, but if you know anything about me, I was still leery about Judas and his situation. I decided to take one day at a time, stay in the present and watch how things played out.

Actually, It was playing out quite well. Two months into this "new us," I still hadn't met the mother of this beautiful baby girl. Again, one day at time helps me stay present and for Judas and me, our relationship was going smoothly. We continued to enjoy one another, and he started coming around a little more frequently when my children were home.

School had resumed for the new semester, so they were home daily, and Judas was there so much that there were days I thought that he might as well live there. It wasn't in my plans then, but I had no complaints about his presence. Life felt good, and I was having fun, despite all the moving parts.

While I was enjoying every day with Judas to the fullest, I still regularly attended Sunday services at the church Peter, and I belonged to and attended together. I looked forward to hearing the teaching from the woman of God the coming Sunday. If anything was ever bothering me, by the time I left Sunday service, it was over with, and I was no longer bothered. This woman could preach, teach, deliver, and chastise you all in one service. Oh, and did I mention she delivers the true raw Word of God? A true messenger of God! If she speaks it, it comes to pass. Whether it be a warning or an instruction, it shall come to pass.

1 Corinthians 14:33

For God is not the author of

confusion but of peace, as in all the churches of the saints.

5 THE WARNING

Chapter 5

THERE IS ONE SUNDAY, TO THIS DAY, THAT I WILL NEVER forget. Praise service was always exceptional and on occasion, comical in a good way. The EODM choir sets the tone and invites the LORD's presence to every service, whether it be in the storefront or on the sidewalk. There was no way that anyone was falling asleep in that church. The energy level was too great, and the anointing was too heavy. After the choir turns the praise and worship all the way up, the church would stand for the introduction and arrival of the Apostle of the house.

On this Sunday, the Apostle sought out, delivered, and conquered as usual. The house was packed, and the word went forward like never before. Just as she began to give the closing of the sermon, she called me to the pulpit. She stepped down from the podium and looked directly into my eyes. As I stood there looking at her, she said to me, "I don't know who "HE" is, but GOD said NO, GOD said that is not your husband."

I was shocked, amazed and frankly a little confused. Who told this woman I was dating someone? Clearly not me, because I did not tell anyone in the church that I had moved on and was entertaining someone after Peter and I broke up. I was not at all embarrassed by it, but I was shocked that she knew I was seeing someone. She said a few more things that I forgot immediately because I was caught off guard.

When she was done, I politely returned to my seat and all of Peter's family's eyes were on me. I just smiled at them and said, "I ain't on nothing." Now everybody in the congregation knew since the pastor said it. I figured I would just come clean about it. After the service, Peter's family and I gathered outside as we usually do and everyone kept repeating what the Apostle had said to me, "He is not your husband." Peter's family knew that he and I was finished however, they were glad to hear that whoever "he" is, he was not my husband (the whole time, hoping Peter and I Re-kindle). I continued to laugh it off and eventually we said our goodbyes and headed home until the next week.

Once I got home, I called Lasagna and told her about the amusement of the day. We laughed about it and never considered it to be an issue. After all, Judas and I were nowhere close to talking about marriage. Honestly, from that day forward, I subconsciously let that "premonition" go.

Judas and I continued dating for the next four months, becoming more exclusive. During this time, he purchased his parents' previous family home and told me that he couldn't wait until we could be together someday under the same roof. He said that he was tired of us being in two different places running back and forth to see each other. I said that my lease was up at the end of the year and if he wanted me to, I would pass on the renewal and move in with him while he finished the work on his place. My thoughts were that we could go from there. He agreed that it was a good idea. Three months later, my children and I moved in, and everyone seemed good with it.

The move was swift and smooth. I gave away practically a full three bedroom, living room and dining room furniture set to include all accessories with the exclusion of one of the children's bunk bed sets. Judas and I had already determined we would buy everything new, so I got rid of all my stuff that was in excellent condition with no signs of wear and tear. It wasn't a big deal to me. Hell, there's this thing about me. Whenever I start anything over, I want everything new. A new look with all new meanings. When I left my first marriage, I didn't want or take anything other than clothing. When I got my new place, I bought everything new, and all those practically new things from the previous life were given away.

After a few weeks of settling in, all was well in our house, or so I thought. Judas' baby momma somehow got word that he bought the house and would constantly call and try to make her way there. He was good at spinning her off for whatever reason, but on this day, she called and heard my children in the background. Now, I was standing next to Judas because we were working on the house together, and heard Luci say, "Who is that? Whose kids are those?" Annoyed, he rolled his eyes and puckered his brow. "Them Felecia's kids."

The phone went silent and that was the end of that conversation. A few hours later, she started calling back, but Judas wouldn't answer her calls. He said he wasn't about to explain anything to her because it wasn't her business. He said he didn't have time for her drama. I was glad to hear that.

For the next year or so, life with Luci was just a tad short of being something like a circus. She tried every trick in the book to interrupt our household. Everything from late night phone calls about the baby being sick to crying her heart out to me, saying Judas led her to believe that they were getting back together to raise their child together as a family.

Sometimes, I wanted to go back to the old me, a.k.a. Skanless Fee, and kick some doors in, take names and ask questions later. I have since outgrown my young adult behavior, but I hope and pray it doesn't ever have to manifest again. Although I made my presence felt and demanded respect, I was surely tried, tested and certified by both of them in the area of pushing all of my buttons when it came to their co-parenting shenanigans.

On the flip side of things, the children and I settled in well and life continued to go on. One thing about Judas, to say the least, is that he is very good at convincing you to believe his story, regardless of the facts. Aside from all the drama and accusations from Luci, Judas said that he was "tired of waiting" and was ready to take our relationship to another level.

We went out to celebrate his birthday, and that is when the discussion came about. The next morning when we were in our right sober mind, we talked about it further. Our conversation led to the decision that we would get married. We picked a date six months out, which happened to be the week of spring break.

So, I know what you're thinking. That pastor said, "He is not your husband." Well believe it or not, at the time, that never crossed my mind. In fact, I stopped going to my home church. I had a change of heart about socializing with my church family, and my friends. I felt a certain amount of respect for my new relationship, so I focused on things at home. Together, within six months, Judas and I planned, financed, and coordinated our wedding. Everything was perfect, and I was soon to be Mrs. Felecia Isharat.

On March 15, 2008, life as my children and I knew it shifted. It was on this day that I became the wife of Mr. Judas Isharat. I was prepared to become a wife again and took great pleasure in representing and carrying my new husband's name. This was my second marriage, and my goal was to make it better than the first and hopefully the last. I made a vow to myself to not give up so easily, even if adversity strikes. This was it. This man was older, wiser, had experience as a husband and knew how to provide for his house. So, we should be good.

When it comes to being a wife and mother, I take pride in my commitment and honor to bring harmony into our home. Respect is a priority. I give respect and get respect. Everyone is happy. I am by no means a perfect person and I have learned that my communication efforts and techniques could use some adjusting, and so I did. I committed to being a better wife and exercise patience when adversity strikes. I committed to checking myself and recognizing my flaws and what I can do differently to potentially experience my happily ever after with this marriage.

Even though I'm not superstitious, there were so many things falling apart the very morning of the ceremony. First, my hair stylist of 17 years was nowhere to be found. We were together the night before sitting in the shop in hopes of getting at least one or two of the bridesmaids' hair done. That didn't happen, so it was agreed and understood that she would get all the heads done in the early morning before the wedding. After two hours and constant calls to her phone, I knew I had to venture out somewhere else. Without knowing where to start, I called anyone who may have known someone, who may be up and available that early in the morning to get the girls and my hair done. I could not believe that this was happening to me the morning of my wedding. How could someone I've known for eighteen years stand me up on one of the most important days of my life? I was in total disbelief. After finally getting some random young lady to jump in and get the girls and my hair done, I was now on my way home to get dressed.

It was one hour before showtime, and we were just leaving the hair salon. I drove about 100 miles per hour speed, to get to the other side of town with hopes that I would not be late for my special day. I had house guests, bridesmaids, family, and friends all at my house helping to make this day special; but sadly, that experience was stolen from me. Once I arrived at the house, everything had to be carried out with a sense of urgency. I was running out of time.

Every cell phone in the house was ringing. Guests were arriving at the chapel and being seated, as the ceremony was soon to be starting. Meanwhile, I was at the house still putting on makeup and trying to get dressed and making sure my girls were doing the same. Thank GOD for all the ladies that were at the house with me. Some combed my babies' hair, while others helped the bridesmaids get themselves together.

Make-up has never been a desire or thing to do for me, so I trusted my application of it to my best girlfriend, Lasagne, who could do wonders with it and had the experience of making it look so easy. Hair done, nails done, makeup flawless and now it was time to slip into my beautiful dress. The closer I got to being ready, the more the phones rang. All finishing touches were done, the limo was outside waiting, and I was finally getting over this sense of urgency and the quivering in my stomach. Just as everyone was about to walk out the bedroom where I was getting dressed, Lasagna gestured to me to look down and there was smeared MAKEUP on my dress. "What The Hell?" was all I could say at that point. As careful as we were during the process of application, this was becoming a nightmare right before my eyes. At that moment the phone rang again, and it was Judas on the line. "Where y'all at, what y'all doing?" he asked in that casual tone of his. All the guests were there, and the ceremony was now one hour behind schedule. I had just calmed down, feeling somewhat relaxed, but then my anxiety level went through the roof. Without breaking a sweat or at least letting them see me sweat, I kept it moving.

We finally made it to the chapel and the ceremony didn't skip a beat. Except to say that it was two hours behind schedule. YES, two hours. Everyone was restless, yet they were beautiful and full of joy; they were happy! The atmosphere was bright, and love was in the air. With all the obstacles that I stumbled over, the moment of matrimony was perfect! That is, until the best man presented Judas with his ring. He looked at the ring and noticed that one of the diamonds was missing from the setting. *What The Hell?* The only other thing that could go wrong was if Judas changed his mind and didn't want to get married. By that point, my mind was all over the place and I was starting to think, what could possibly be next?

At some point, the nuptials were exchanged, and we were then pronounced Mr. and Mrs. Judas Isharat. While I was happy and full of joy, I was also a bit disappointed because everything was rushed since I was running so far behind on time.

From taking pictures to dinner and dancing with our guests, everything was done in a hurry. It was unfortunate that we missed out on the moments that were supposed to be captured, priceless and savored for a lifetime. Through it all, we made the best of it. We were surrounded by friends and family from near and far and we were honored they joined us for this special celebration of love. We were now one, 'til death do us part.

Mark 10:8

...and the two shall become one flesh;

so then they are no longer two, but one flesh.

THE FOUNDATION

Chapter 6

ONCE THE WEDDING WAS BEHIND US, AND THE honeymooN was over, life as we knew it was in full effect. We all seemed to be adapting well and looking forward to abundance and overflow as our due portion. Our friends sometimes would refer to us as the "power couple." We had promising career jobs, our children were doing well and every day we intended to live and enjoy life to its fullest; not to mention, we looked damn good together!

Life as I knew it was good. Not perfect, but good. If something adverse was going on in our household, we kept it in the house and dealt with it accordingly. As much as possible, we kept our disagreements between us as a couple. There are no perfect couples (unless you're the Obama's) that I've yet to see conquer marriage without trials and tribulations. The quickest way to tear down your house is to invite other people's opinion into it.

The summer of 2008 was in full effect, including a family reunion from Judas' mom's side of the family. He always looked forward to these celebrations. Each reunion year, it is hosted by a different family household from a different state. Each gathering is special in its own way and hails to its own highlights that will remain in your memory for years to come. With most of the family raised up from the south, the food is always soulful and abundant. The games, slide shows, talent shows, music and acknowledgments were all perfectly entertaining. I love family gatherings, socializing and having fun with people around me. There's so much bad stuff going on in the world today that enjoying your loved ones should be a daily priority.

As often as we could, Judas and I would plan somewhere for the two of us to go. Sometimes it was just a weekend getaway, other times it was a week-long vacation with friends. Both sides of his family are huge, so there was always something going on somewhere. My children were teenagers during this time, had their own agendas and most times didn't want to roll with us on our escapades. There were a few times, however, that they had to stay back as a punishment for not following through on something or doing something they were told not to do.

They used to say we did old folks' stuff, so most times they were glad to stay behind. After going to Mississippi, a couple of times, they decided they didn't want to go anymore because the weather was too hot, and the bugs were too big. I think that long drive played a part as well. Now that I think about it, maybe they just wanted to be home alone to do their own thing, huh? Well, whatever they did or didn't do, they held it down and cleaned up before we got back.

Watching my family grow was such a joy for me. My children were doing well in school with both academics and athletics. The oldest and youngest children were excelling with honors while my middle child was tearing up basketball courts everywhere throughout the public school system. This child of mine has the potential to be the next great WNBA player. When I tell you that my daughter eats, sleeps and drinks basketball, it is the truth. It is truly her passion, and she gives it her all. Now, if I could just keep her focused, she would be great.

With Judas remodeling our home, we were all learning new

things and how to plaster, mud, paint, stain and whatever else you could think of when it comes to renovations. By the time the house was complete, we all had contributed and sacrificed blood, sweat and tears to beautifying our house and making it a home. Each room was detailed with its own color scheme and ambiance. Yet, as you walked through the house, all the rooms' schemes came together, and the colors coordinated and set the tone for peace and tranquility. While the neighborhood sometimes got a bad rap, whenever guests would enter our home, they were amazed at how beautiful it was.

When it came to the outside of the house, I left all that to Judas. I do not, by any means, have that green thumb gift of planting, gardening, and landscaping. So, Judas would cut, trim, fertilize and water the grass. I mean, he would have that grass on point! I don't mind raking leaves and shoveling snow, but lawn care is not my forté.

While Judas was cutting and trimming the lawn, I was doing the clean-up. I would bag up all the grass he cut, remove the weeds, and set up the water hose for him. I loved that it was a shared effort in keeping our house and landscaping in pristine condition. Inside and out, our place was nearly perfect. We took pride in the design and upkeep of our home. As much as we could, we enjoyed opening our doors to family and friends. We loved to host family events and holidays, watch parties, couples' dinners, Keno or simply just having friends over for cocktail hour.

While I enjoyed having family and friends visit, sitting on the front or back porch enjoying the fresh air was my favorite. After a long day's work, Judas and I would grab our beverage of choice and share our workday shenanigans, as we laugh and listen to music sometimes until the late hours of the night.

Summer is my favorite season, but it never seems long enough. It feels like just a few good weeks then - boom, it's over. We usually end the summer with some sort of birthday celebration for Judas. During the first week of September, there is guaranteed to be a BBQ in honor of him. Every year the theme is different and better than the previous one.

The crowd grew larger and larger each year. Family, friends, and friends of friends would come out and party with us, with the last guest usually leaving about 4 a.m. Labor Day weekend was a sure hit on Bell Street.

One year, the party was so large and carried on into the next morning, that our neighbors called the police on us for disturbing the peace. I think it was the 4 a.m. 'live and in color' Karaoke shenanigans that drove them to the edge and forced that phone call... lol.

As sure as I am cute and slim, thick... Yep, I said it: "slim thick," (Says Mr. Portwood) summer came and went like overnight. Fall season pushed us back into reality. No more enjoying the night air on the porch. No more BBQ's. No more watching the kids run up and down the block, and most of all, no more evenings sitting around doing nothing.

When it came time for the kids to get ready for school, they weren't really enthused about it. I, on the other hand, enjoyed getting them prepared to take on the next level of education and accountability. With two teenagers in high school and one child in elementary school, we had our work cut out for us. We had already been successful and got the oldest girl through high school with honors, so this school year should be a little less stressful for us. Meanwhile, still in our honeymoon phase, together Judas and I were building a foundation and planting seeds into our children that would grow and flourish for years to come.

That year, school was a success. Now, as much as I hate the fall and winter seasons, I love the holidays. Thanksgiving is the children's favorite because they love the food and fellowship with family. The kids have pretty much outgrown Christmas, but oh! how we love New Year's Eve! Judas and I really didn't care about being out on New Year's Eve because we had some memorable celebrations in our own home. Being home allowed the children to partially participate in the festivities, so that was a plus. That year's party was definitely an experience for the children and full of fun.

Despite all shenanigans, it took our not-so-joyful neighbors to again call the boys in blue and have it shut down. I suppose it was because it sounded like Vietnam was behind our house; some may have been disturbed, while others were just party poopers.

When I tell you the whole 8th district police department invaded our party, believe me. It was the funniest scene I had ever witnessed up, close and in person. It happened so fast. My bestie was calling me on the phone to check and see what was happening just minutes before the officers arrived. Lasagne said, "Kev just heard on the police scanner that they have y'all house surrounded by officers due to rapid gun fire."

Before I had a chance to announce it to everyone in the house, to warn those who were heading to the back of the house, the boys in blue were storming through the front door. While it may be funny now, it surely wasn't at the time. Apparently, my brother-in-law was headed out the front door to go home and as soon as he opened the door, he was ambushed by the cops. He immediately dropped to his knees and put his hands behind his head. "Officer," he said. "Officer, I'm leaving. I didn't do anything." Now, you are talking about funny things, LORD help me! I still laugh about this today.

The officers politely escorted my brother-in-law back into the house and swarmed the place. Luckily, the one guest who was in the garage was able to conceal armory and ammunition before the cops made it out there. Meanwhile, it was pure mayhem. The police were everywhere. Most of the guests in the house stood still and watched as others felt the need to fuel the fire.

My son-in-law, whose father is a cop, could not get with the officers storming into his dad's house and ordering everyone to sit down. He verbally took on one of the cops and made sure he let him know they had no right to be there, and they were not running anything up in there. As the argument escalated, our 150 lb. Cane Corso emerged from the laundry room area of the house and went head on in the direction of the chaos. The moment that the officer saw Kimora (the dog), he drew his weapon and yelled, "Someone get this $@#&ing dog! Get this dog! I swear I will shoot it!"

With my son-in-law screaming at the police, "You better not shoot my $@#&ing dog," the chaos grew to epic proportions! Finally, one of the cousins stepped forward and commanded Kimora to back off and she went back into the laundry area without incident. The whole scene was like straight out of a B-movie, with complete foolery and chaos.

Meanwhile, upstairs, the sergeant on duty was questioning

Judas and me about the location of the weapons that were being fired off.

The sergeant was stern and forthright. "I know there are guns in this house, where are they?" This went on for a bit, back and forth as Judas tried to explain to them that the only weapon, he had was his duty weapon. "I'm Officer Judas Isharat, 2nd District," he stated.

Well, that announcement held no weight with the sergeant. He instructed his officers to continue searching for weapons. It wasn't until one of the other officers pulled Judas to the side and said, "Hey, give us something and we will leave. So, Judas thought that would be easy enough. He folded and gave the officer an old military weapon he had stored away many years ago. Thinking that would be the end, the sergeant looked at it and said, "Well, who's going to take the rap for this?"

I thought for a minute. Judas is an officer so he can't say it belongs to him, it could cost him his job. If I say it's mine, it won't cost me my job but may scar my clean record which I will justify in the courts. So, guess what? I told the officer it was my weapon, and I would take the rap for it. No way was I going to let Judas lose his career job.

That being said.... the officers recorded my information, ended their search for more weapons, and left the house.

Needless to say the New Year's Eve party ended, but not until we laughed for another hour about how my brother-in-law broke down to his knees, and how the police were going to shoot our dog. If ever I laughed until I cried, this was the time.

No paperwork or report was given to us, and I never heard of the incident again until years later. Judas came home from work on a random day and said he was called into the office regarding this incident, and it warranted a one-day suspension, and he complied with the reprimand. He said he was told that with the suspension, it was settled and would never come up again. THANK GOD!!!!!

These are the times I live for. To live, love, build and create memories with my family.

1 Timothy 6:18-19

...instruct them to do good, to be rich in good works,

to be generous and ready to share,

storing up for themselves the treasure

of a good foundation for the future,

so that they may take hold of that which is life indeed.

7 THE BREACH

Chapter 7

HAPPY NEW YEAR! The New Year 2009 began with great fanfare; there were many new things on the horizon. It came in with a blast and the Isharat's New Year Extravaganza was talked about for years to come. As January settled in, I was on the lookout for "The Next." That is, whatever life had to offer me that was good. The next good thing.

Life has taught me that in a blink of an eye, everything around you can change. People change, the way people treat you can change and if you're not paying attention, the people around you will cause *you* to change. Now, change sometimes is good, but just because it's good, that doesn't mean it's good for you.

The beginning of the year was very promising. I had a new husband, new family, new face to our home and I was experiencing a new transition in my career. I was working for one of the largest health systems in the state and I which allowed me to expand my knowledge and clinical application. For me, this was caused to celebrate! As we did all too often, Judas and I gathered with family and friends to spend time laughing, dancing, drinking, and celebrating my next venture.

Judas has an aunt who always opens her home to us. She loves it when family and friends visit to enjoy and love one another. At his Aunt Jazzy's house, there was never a dull moment. Jazzy enjoyed putting the spotlight on whoever was celebrating something special. That was her way; she made each person feel equally celebrated and loved. It was beautiful.

Did I mention that she LOVED her Judas and Felecia? Oh, yeah! Jazzy always reminded us that she was happy that we were husband and wife. Almost all of Judas' family and those around us encouraged us, commended us and wished us well in our marriage. Although they were Judas' family, I loved and respected each of them as if they were my own. To share and celebrate with them was priceless.

Like clockwork, we were at Aunt Jazzy's house, celebrating my new nursing venture for several hours. As the evening came to an end and everyone was saying their goodbye's no sooner than the door closed as the last person left, we were already planning our next gathering, all while cleaning up from this rendezvous. All the furniture was put back in place, food leftovers were disposed of, and the garbage was taken out. Now if the DJ would just stop playing the music, we could all go home. The closer I got to the door, the more the

DJ played my favorite songs. Music is my therapy; add a cocktail or two and I'm all in… LET'S PARTY!

Now I understand the reason why liquor is also referred to as "spirits."

I have experienced, as well as witnessed, the effects that liquor has on those who consume way too much. It's all good during the consumption, but the later effect is sometimes toxic in too many ways to count. Some people in a drunken state turn to anger, aggression, sadness, delusion, or rage while under the influence, whereas others may be happy, loving, outgoing, even promiscuous, and free spirited. Liquor (spirits) seemingly remains dormant until something excites or triggers a manifestation. I know you know what I mean.

Yes, it's true. Once we got home from a fantastic night with family, everyone was winding down. The children were safe and sound asleep in their room. Judas and I showered and prepared for a good night's sleep. Then, out of nowhere, it happened. Judas insinuated that one of his cousins was "looking at me" in such a way. Laughing, I replied, "Judas please, no one is looking at me like that. Your family is my family, and we were all just having a good time laughing together and having fun".

Well, that was not the way Judas saw things. He continued to carry on with what he believed happened. Soon enough, my mood shifted from happy to WTF?! All I wanted to do was flop into bed and slip into sleepy time.

Judas had other ideas. He wanted to have sex. Well now, pissing me off will NEVER get you sex; and probably for days to come.

How can you intentionally create a negative environment and then switch it up because you want to be intimate? I have not yet fully understood that mess. Let's be clear. This wasn't a "break up to make up" scenario. By now my patience had diminished, and I was in no mood to put up with his unwarranted bad behavior. I felt like he was low-key accusing me of something. So, my "no" to sex was SOLID. It was just not going to happen.

Then BOOM! Without warning, Judas flipped me on my back in bed.

He straddled over top of my body, attempting to kiss me. As I tossed and turned, telling him to get off me and rejecting his kissing attempts, he head butt me.

"Are you f*cking serious?!" I yelled. Even he looked stunned. I shoved him off me, and we both realized that there was blood streaming down my face.

As I got up to go into the bathroom to look at myself in the mirror, my kids showed up at our bedroom door. My oldest daughter asked, "Momma, what's wrong?" I rushed into the bathroom as fast as I could and clapped back, "Nothing baby. Go back to bed. Momma's fine." Apparently, they were awakened by the commotion in our bedroom. This was the worst and last thing I ever wanted my children to have to experience. Domestic violence!

With only a small amount of blood and a tiny break of skin across the bridge of my nose, I cleaned myself up and went back into the bedroom. Judas was apologetic and said he didn't mean to do it. I told him how upset I was and that I wanted to be left alone. I climbed in bed, straddled my pillow, closed my eyes, and tried to go to sleep. With all the hell Judas had in him, he had the

69 | THE COST OF DISOBEDIENCE

nerve to lay in bed next to me and put his arms around my body to comfort me while he fell asleep.

My mind was racing, and I felt shaken to the core. How could he dare do that to me? The longer I stewed on it, the angrier I got. I knew the alcohol played a part in Judas' behavior, so I tried to sleep it off, knowing full well that it will be the first thing I attempt to process the next morning. Never in a million years would I have thought that my husband would do something like this to me. What stirred this degree of anger in him? Was it the rejection of me not kissing him? Was it the anger of me not having sex with him? Either way, domestic violence is never, ever acceptable.

As days passed, the tiny cut across my nose turned into a hideous-looking black eye. Each day it turned darker and darker, and I couldn't stand to look at myself in the mirror. I was that poster woman for abuse. Of course, my children were aware of everything going on and started asking questions and showing anger and hostility about what happened. I want you to know that I have always been exceptionally careful about the people I brought into my home. This was something they had never encountered before, and they were confused. I managed to bite the bullet and tell them it was an accident and that I was okay. I'm certain they never believed me because it took over a week before I noticed them speaking their one-word answers back to

Judas. Same house, no communication to their stepfather. They showed their loyalty to me and that is a beautiful thing. Of course, I never discussed my marital problems with my children, but they just knew. They are always watching; remember that. I understood their position. Somehow, Judas had no idea how much it affected them.

Well, the clock kept ticking, the hours kept passing, the days sped by and life continued moving forward.

... and there was good news and bad news for me. The good news? I had a new position and had orientation on a beautiful Monday morning in February. I was excited to be stepping into new territory. I knew I was ready to conquer. The bad news? I still had my black eye. At the time I wondered, *how do I start a new job with a black eye? Do I pass up this once-in-a-lifetime opportunity or do I put my big girl panties on, along with my dark sunglasses and take my place in orientation?* You got it. I got up, dressed up and showed up. Mid-winter generally has no sunshine. Yet, there I was, sitting in a classroom for eight long hours with shades on. Make it make sense.

It was a week-long class as usual; introductions, speakers, presen-ters and getting to know our colleagues. There were some familiar faces at the orientation, and I knew it would be a matter of time before I would be face to face with them, of course, with my sunglasses on. I maintained my disguise and blended it into my daily outfits. However, we all have that one person who has to ask that one question you don't want to answer: "Why do you have your sunglasses on in here?" I was ready. "These are not sunglasses, they are prescription glasses with a dark tint," I said. "This is how I sleep in class and the speaker can't see my eyes closed!" I tried to brush it off as no big deal. Did she believe me? Probably not, but it never came up again.

On the home front, things eventually got a little less stressful every day. Life was moving forward, slowly but surely. Judas apologized for his actions on a couple occasions and vowed to never do anything to hurt me again. After a while I forgave Judas, and it appeared that the kids were coming around and living life as children are supposed to. Children should never have to live in an environment that forces them to feel emotions that they are not yet able to process. As parents, we must set positive examples, then mold, nurture and teach love and kindness to our children.

Moving forward, my hope was that my family would overcome and heal from this experience. It was something that should have never happened. Our life together had just begun and there was so much more we had to look forward to.

I Corinthians 13:6-7

"It (love) does not rejoice in wrongdoing, but rejoices with the truth. Love bears all things, believes all things, hopes all things, endures all things."

8 THE SEPARATION

Chapter 8

TO BE HONEST, IT HAD BEEN A VERY EVENTFUL AND SATISFYING first year of marriage. Between going to work every day and combining our families as one, I was so ready for the summer to roll back around the children were flourishing in school and my aspiring WNBA player, (my youngest daughter) was doing her thing on the basketball team. I settled in with my new job, and I remember one day saying to myself, "I can't remember when I have been this happy!"

Judas and I were doing great, and the children were again, warming up to him. I sensed, though, that they really did not count on him for anything. In their minds, he wasn't even close to receiving the Stepfather of the Year Award. My children have never had a male figure discipline them. Although I have been married and given birth to children in my first marriage, it was always by default that I would issue the discipline and correct my children. Not that my previous husband didn't have the authority to do so; he just didn't want to, and I was perfectly fine with that.

Judas, on the other hand, was strict. I believe it is because of his career path. He demanded order and sometimes he didn't know how to communicate properly or realize when he was crossing the line. Often, I would have to say, "Hey, Judas, please leave your work at work," because he would raise his voice, break stuff and demand that things be done now, not when you want to do it. Now, the girls did not have any problems following house rules, doing chores, or even trying to help and learn new things. However, Judas' authoritative and aggressive approach sometimes made it a somewhat uncomfortable situation for everyone.

THE COST OF DISOBEDIENCE

On the flip side, Judas was giving, caring, concerned and supportive within our household. Whenever the children or I needed something, he made sure we got it. Even though we were both financially stable, he was committed to making sure we had what we needed. Together, we shared the living expenses for the home, which included the mortgage, utilities, insurance and any renovations. If it was something we needed and I didn't get it first, Judas would take care of it. I knew in my heart that he wanted the best for us. He wanted our family to succeed and prosper. Unfortunately, life threw us a curveball that was far above what we could reach.

The events that took place on a beautiful late summer afternoon of July 8, 2009, is embedded in my photographic memory. I can summon it at will. Judas and I were sitting on the porch, sipping our favorite Cognac, and enjoying our moments together. Soon, we noticed my 16-year-old daughter walking down the street. She was coming home from after-school practice, and she greeted us on the porch with a lot of excitement. We asked her how her day was and what was going on that made her so happy. She told us that the basketball coach invited her to play basketball in a summer league in Florida.

Of course, as parents do, we started asking questions like, who's paying for this? What's the cost? Who is attending?

Will there be parents or chaperones allowed? And when is this supposed to happen?

My daughter knew just enough details at the time that Judas and I congratulated her, and I was the first to say, "Yes!" I know my daughter's commitment to basketball, and I love to see her out there on the court dominating and executing the game.

Judas also loved to watch her play. However, he had one condition for her going to the summer league. He said, "If your grades are good, we will pay for you to go. If your grades aren't right, you can't go." Then he paused for a couple of seconds. "All right?"

My baby girl's face immediately dropped, and her momentum faded. She walked into the house mumbling that her grades were good, but from the look on her face, I had a feeling they weren't. We would know in a week when report cards came out.

Judas and I continued having cocktails and listening to music on the front porch. I suppose our energy was contagious because my baby girl came back out and mingled with us for a while. The days were never long enough. We were out on that porch until the wee hours of the morning. I didn't have to work the next day and Judas never needed eight hours of sleep before work. Most times, he was good with four to six hours. Eventually we called it a night and headed to bed.

The next morning, Judas was at work, and I was home doing my normal routine: cleaning, laundry, organizing and preparing for dinner. The children were at school, so this was "my time." While I was being productive, cleaning things relaxes me, if it makes sense. I'm big on order and organization and there's nothing better than a clean house.

At about 11:00 that morning, I got a text from a number I didn't recognize. The text said, "Mommy, I need to tell you something." I responded with, "Who is this?" It was my 16-year-old daughter. I texted back, "What's wrong?" Her response was, "Judas is touching me." My heart fell into my stomach. I was nauseous and weak; I was shaking. I texted, "What are you saying?" She responded, "He is doing stuff to me".

I was in a state of shock. I felt dizzy. Wobbly. Out of control. I did not want to believe the text I just read, but I pulled myself together enough to text back and minutes later, I was on my way to pick her up from school. I threw on some clothes and headed out the door. I was crying. At the stop sign. At the red light. In front of me. My tears of betrayal blurred the entire drive.

Once I drove up to the school, I pulled myself together because I didn't want my baby girl to see me in such a state. I walked inside the high school's main office to sign her out and told the staff she would be back tomorrow. We left the school and headed straight to the hospital.

Driving my daughter to the hospital because she told me she was raped by my husband, her stepfather, is the most heart-wrenching thing that I have ever done in my life.

I had questions. How? When? Where did this happen? Each question I asked was very SPECIFIC and some, I asked her to elaborate. I remember her saying the last incident was a couple months prior. I remember her saying it he would be inappropriate with her while I was away at work. I remember her saying he said inappropriate things to her in the basement of our home. While I heard everything, she stated to me, I couldn't grasp my mind around any of it. I was totally in shock. I never doubted what she told me; I just needed to be clear on what she was saying. With each question I asked, there were 100 more things relating to that question running through my mind all at the same time. I found myself in the kind of shock that isn't connected to any reality around me. I was angry and heartbroken. My daughter is telling me she was violated. How did I not protect my child from what she is saying happened to her?

Coming from a home of childhood sexual abuse, I always knew that my children were my number one priority, and I would never put them in harm's way. I swore that if any of my children ever told me that someone violated them, I knew that I would be going to hell or jail for my actions.

Pushing my anger aside, I gathered my composure and offered my daughter my deepest sympathy and regret. I explained to her that she could tell me anything. I encouraged her to express what she was feeling. I truly wanted to know how she was dealing with this. It was devastating. She eventually said that she was okay and didn't want to go to the hospital. I told her that once she was checked by a doctor, I would bring her home. Although she stated it was a couple of months ago since Judas violated her, I still felt the need to take her to get checked out. I wasn't thinking in the realm of DNA collection, I was thinking More-so about her overall health and wellness. During the drive to the hospital, she vowed to me that she was not voluntarily sexually active in no way for or fashion. With that being said, there were particular questions that I knew the doctors could answer.

When we got to the hospital, I told the security officer at the check-in desk that my daughter needed to see a doctor; he asked me why and so I told him. We were called within minutes to see the female doctor on duty. She assured me she would take good care of my baby. Due to privacy, HIPAA laws and the nature of the case, the doctor said she needed me to leave the room after the examination. She said she had to speak with my daughter alone. Whatever they needed me to do, I did. I had to make sure my baby was all right.

Later that day, Judas was off duty and calling my phone, blowing it up. The very sight of seeing his number on my caller ID sent me into a weak and nervous state. I didn't know if I should answer it or just let him call 100 more times and ignore him. Eventually, I answered. "Hey baby, where are you?" he asked.

"I'm at the hospital with Babygirl," I replied. Without saying another word, he said, "I'm on my way, where ya'll at'?" So, I told him. So, you're probably wondering, "WHY"? Why did I tell him? As a healthcare provider and a mandated reporter, I knew when he stepped foot through the door, he would be arrested.

By then, the doctor called me to the exam room and let me sit with my daughter. I asked if she was all right. With her hands laying behind her head as she lay flat on the bed she said, "Yes, Mommy. I'm okay."

The doctor spoke with me alone to give me her findings from the examination. In a sense, I'm relieved, but I'm also scared, angry and confused. So many people were soon put in front of me, asking me the most important questions of my life. I talked to the police, social services, and several doctors, and at any minute I thought my body would give out and I would collapse. Just when I thought I pulled myself together, I saw Judas walk through the hospital door. As soon as he called my name, the police swarmed him and placed him inside the police car waiting outside.

"Felecia!" he called out. "Felecia, what's going on?"

I could not think of anything to say to him. I lost all words. I watched the squad car pull away with my husband in the back seat. I was still in shock. I walked back into the hospital, found the nearest bathroom, sat there on the floor and cried. Before long, I heard my name called, so I rushed back to the emergency room area. I was told I could take my daughter home and that the authorities would be in contact with me. I pulled myself together and took my baby girl home.

When we got home, I made several attempts to get Babygirl to talk and share her emotions, feelings, concerns, and fears with me. She said she had none. While I know everyone handles trauma differently, I felt that this was something that we needed to discuss. We are talking about my husband, her stepfather. I know first-hand that this is not something that a person holds inside or brushes off like it never happened. Given the transparent relationship I have with my children, I knew for certain that they fully believed that they could discuss anything with me, good, bad, ugly, or otherwise.

As hours passed, I told the other kids what was going on. They were all upset, scared, angry and in total disbelief. I did my best to comfort them and reassure them that everything would be all right. Since Babygirl wouldn't talk to me about what happened, I figured I would just fall back and wait until she was ready. I kept a watchful eye on her, studied her and tried to get into her head. I wanted to make sure she was not internalizing her emotions or pain and trying to deal with it alone. It was really strange to me, though; she seemed to be her normal self.

By the end of the night, every Chicagoland T.V. station was at my front door. When your husband is a police officer and accused of molesting or raping his stepdaughter, the word gets around fast. There were so many cameras outside my house and set up down the block, it was like a movie shoot. The knocks on the door were intimidating and the reporters were shouting questions without me ever acknowledging them. The children were scared and before I knew it, they were hysterical. I ran around the house closing all the blinds and making sure all the doors were locked. I told all the kids to stay in the basement, and that everything was going to be all right. It was heartbreaking for me to see my children so scared and shaken by the cameras, the crowd, and the pounding on the door.

Again, something about this is strange. All my other children are freaking out and Babygirl is playing a video game. I couldn't help it. I thought, LORD, *help me! Either this is one strong young lady, or her mind block game is tight.* Might I add, blocking out things can be very dangerous, and I didn't want that type of heavy mental stress on her.

The next thing I knew, Babygirl blurted out, "If I knew all this was gonna happen, I wouldn't have said anything."

I couldn't believe what she just said.

"Why are you not talking about this?" I pleaded. "Your sisters and brother and I are working through this, and we are all worried about you." I waited for her to say something, but nothing left her lips. So, I continued. "We are not even worried about Judas. If he did what you said he did, he will get what he deserves."

I was struggling to process what had happened. I felt guilty. I was numb. *How did I miss this? I must protect my children. What do I do now?*

Judas was detained for a week because of Babygirl's allegations; then out of the blue, he called to say that he had been released on bond and would be staying at a family member's house. It was not far from where we lived, but the condition of bond was that he couldn't come to the house because the kids were there. He asked if he could talk to me and if I could bring him some clothes. With much dread and reluctance, I did. It was very apparent that being detained had taken a toll on him, mentally and physically. I couldn't bear to look at him in that weak condition.

When I dropped off his clothes, he was crying. He never stopped, assuring me that he did not and would never do such a horrible thing like that and he said he had no idea why Babygirl would say such a thing about him.

I listened to every word he breathed out between his tears, but ultimately, I had nothing to say. What was I supposed to say? Hell, I was being generous just bringing him clothes. *Why did I bring him clothes? Why aren't I attempting to take his life at this very minute?* There were some missing pieces and I needed to figure them out. Believe it or not, one of the reasons I was generous enough to bring him clothes, is that the Doctor could not confirm that babygirl was violated, but only that she had been penetrated. Also, taking into her account of behaviors, led me to believe was this some sort of revenge because Judas spoke against her basketball trip.

If I ever needed GOD, now was the time. With having to talk to the investigators, social services and my family asking questions and making assumptions, I needed an outlet for my children and me. We needed to be able to talk to someone; someone who was neutral, someone my kids could be open with and someone who could help them process what was going on around them. I enrolled all of us into family counseling. I will tell you, seeking counseling was the best decision I could have made during that time. I encourage anyone who is dealing with the unexpected in life to consider talking it over with an experienced counselor. However, even before you talk to anyone, remember that GOD will listen, answer, and guide you. He will never leave you, nor forsake you.

Psalms 86:7 says:

In the day of my trouble I shall call upon You,

For You will answer me.

9 THE DESCENT

Chapter 9

JUDAS AND I SPENT THE NEXT YEAR HOUSED APART. This was no way to build our life together amongst the division. All our communication revolved around Babygirl's accusation. After a year of this, I was still trying to hold myself and my children together, mentally, and emotionally. So much happened and so many things took me by surprise; I had no time to crumble. I knew how to keep pushing. I had to do what was best for the wellness and well-being of my family. What I learned in that year living apart from my husband is that you never know your strength until you've been tested.

The case against Judas was coming to an end. According to legal counsel, the investigation revealed that no evidence was found and the statements that were given were conflicting and contradictory. Social Services ended their investigation and closed the case because of inconclusive evidence.

The counseling sessions with the kids and me had reached the expiration date and the counselor said there was no further need to return. I thought the charade was almost over. The authorities offered one last meeting with Babygirl and I to go over the evidence and findings. The meeting was only weeks away and I could tell this was uncomfortable for her She started asking about what the trial would be like.

I tried to explain to her without making her fearful. "There will be a lot of questions, some of them they will ask over and over to try and trip you on your words," I said. "They will probably try to paint a negative picture of you to shade your character or say you are troubled," I warned. "As long as you tell the truth and he did what you said he did, you will be fine," I added. I promised her I would be there the entire time, every time, always and forever.

Babygirl held her head down and then said, "Well, what if I say it never happened?"

Her answer got my attention really quick. "Why would you say that?"

Her sister spoke up next. "What do you mean? It didn't happen?"

Things got serious. "If Judas did it, why would you ever want to retract that statement"? I asked. I told her that this was a severe accusation and if they found out she lied, they could bring charges against her. "I can't tell you what to do, Babygirl. If it happened, then tell the truth. If it didn't happen, then tell the truth."

I was spent. I stood up and walked out of the room.

Sure as the weeks flew by, the meeting had taken place with the proper authorities and all of the evidence and/or lack thereof, was laid out on the table and discussed. During the conclusion of the meeting, it was noted that Babygirl retracted her statement. After that, all charges were immediately dropped, and Judas was free to go back to his home. While I was relieved that what I thought was the worst thing that could have happened, did not happen based on my daughter's final statement, I still had a battle ahead of me. Now that Judas can return home, where does that leave Babygirl? I wondered if it was even fair to him or appropriate that they shelter under the same roof.

The first few weeks of Judas returning home was very awkward, to say the least. The children were on edge and didn't know what to expect from him.

I didn't fully know what to expect either, or even how he would receive my daughter after her false accusation. Yet, he came home with open arms to all the kids. Prior to my husband coming home, I was seeing him and staying nights where he lived until all the papers were processed. So, I wasn't concerned about safety for me or the children. I was more concerned about the mental and emotional effect that it may have on any of them. This was a delicate situation and I had to make sure I protected everyone.

During Judas' first few weeks home, he started getting back to his normal self. Returning to the home he left a year prior was not easy; he knew he had to build bridges, even with Babygirl. He told her that he forgave her and urged her to help get our family back on track. The both of us wanted our family to help each other push the negative out. Well, that sounds almost too good to be true. Oh, how I wish it was that simple and it would have gone that way.

As the days got longer, the time got tougher. With Judas

now home with us, everyone (and their damn mother) had an opinion on how I was handling things. They questioned my morals as a mother, my ability to protect my children and any other cheap shot they thought suitable to discuss. Well, I didn't let it get the best of me. I continued to maintain my position in my house and take care of my family the best way I knew how. I didn't see any of the stone throwers offering a shoulder when I was going through the storm. I don't remember any self-proclaimed family or marriage counselor calling my family, offering a hand or a shotgun when the story broke.

So *now that the dust has cleared, everybody wants to be a HERO. SPARE ME!!*

With much planning and praying, Babygirl went to stay with her paternal uncle to finish out her high school year. For some reason, the counselor felt it was BETTER for her and they wanted her to feel safe. With an open mind, I agreed to let her go. More than anything, I wanted my baby girl to feel okay, safe and finish her school year out strong. Of course, I was judged, and I allowed the shots to be fired behind my back; but somehow, I knew I would get the last laugh, AFTER THIS.

My baby girl was away from home for the first time in her life and as her mother, I had so many mixed emotions about it. She was not out of the state or far away, just out of my nest. I had this beautiful bundle of joy since she was born into this world. When she left, it was hard to adjust to her absence. Once again, I had to put on my big girl panties and continue to function for the other three children I was raising.

Some days were better than others. Trying to also get the kids adjusted to their sister being away was the most complicated. They understood why she wasn't there, but that didn't mean they were okay with it. As a family, we got through it by GOD's grace.

Even with all the negativity that surrounded our family at the time, Judas and I were able to rebuild our relationship with the kids and each other and get back to something normal. I knew that within time, the families who knew part of the story would get over their anger of Judas and me working things out. People would open their arms to Babygirl when they saw her and tell her they still loved her, but there were some who wouldn't, and we were okay with that, too. All was well with me, as long as no one disrespected my baby girl. Every person is entitled to their opinion and to me, it was just that: *Their* Opinion. Period.

Life for the Isharat household got better as days, weeks and months went by. It seemed that we grew closer as a family than ever before. You know that saying, "What doesn't kill you, makes you stronger?" Well, I found that to be true. Judas treated me like the Queen of the Castle. Whatever my heart desired, he would give me. My kids were no longer giving negative attitudes or having behavioral problems. They were just going on with life like teenagers and young adults are supposed to. There were times that I could have never imagined we would be here, after all the hell we endured.

It took a lot of praying, patience, and endurance to keep me sane and guide me in the direction I was going. For all that my children and family went through, the average person in my shoes would have had some form of mental breakdown. I thank GOD. He covered me and equipped me in the battle. I would thank GOD daily for not letting my family fall by the wayside. I prayed daily that GOD allowed me to open my eyes, I promised I would cover my family in prayer and protect them from any evil thing that tried to harm them.

Once I affirmed that I had to protect my family, it was time to get back to the church house. I needed the LORD's covering so that I could fully cover my family. I started going back to church regularly and oh, how I loved it! This was what I needed after many years of not attending services and being fed. I didn't realize how hungry I was.

Psalms 91:1

He that dwelleth in the secret place of the most high shall abide under the shadow of the almighty.

10 THE FALL

Chapter 10

IT HAD BEEN FOUR AND A HALF YEARS (AND COUNTING) since our marriage took a hit, but we both agreed that we rebounded gracefully, and I couldn't have been happier. Although we were not the perfect couple, we were thriving. We were traveling more, stepping outside the box, and conquering our fears. Honestly, we were just trying to live our lives to the fullest. I couldn't ask for anything more.

It is very important that married couples keep outsiders out of their marriage. Who are outsiders? I'm glad you asked. Anyone who is not married to you or your spouse. It's even more crucial to avoid advice from non-married individuals or individuals whose own marriage is out of whack.

All relationships per se' go through some sort of trial and tribulation. Maybe not as serious, but a relationship in some way or another will be tested. How else would you declare the strength of the relationship… unless it's tested? Be careful, though, who you seek out for guidance.

Although life on the home front was good, I was starting to notice that Judas was doing some things differently. He is a man of habit, and while he still caters to me and puts me on a pedestal on every occasion he gets, there was something different going on with him. Now, if you have read this far, you know that I am into my man. I know every little detail of him and about him. Yes, it was still true. So, something was going on and I was not yet sure what it was.

Now, Judas was always on top of his appearance. He cuts his own hair, shaves his own face, and is very particular about how he steps out of the house. I soon noticed he became overly obsessed with his appearance. Usually, he shaves and cuts his hair maybe once a week. I started to notice that he would cut it twice a week and it took longer for him to finish it. Also, I began to realize that he waited until I went to bed at night before he started the process.

As long as Judas and I have been together, he has never been interested in hanging out at bars with his friends. Judas, like me, was more of a homebody, but he would go out if he was invited to a party or event. Now, to just meet at a bar for drinks? That had never been Judas. If ever he was in a bar while we were an item, it was because I was by his side. So, these frequent outings were raising my concern a bit. I trusted him, so I didn't make a fuss about it. I was just curious.

With all the spoiling Judas does to me, he offsets it by doing his second love and hustle, remodeling and updating homes. He's been doing this since I met him and so this was no surprise to me. He even taught me (and the children) many things about home remodeling and construction. What was different, however, were the long hours he was now spending doing projects.

I remember one night; Judas was working on a home about six miles from where we lived. He called to say that he was finishing up his last job. He said, "Baby, can you bring me the shop vac?" Of course, I said yes. He gave me the address, and I took the shop vac to him. He said he would be home as soon as he finished cleaning up the scraps from the project. Okay, great! I went home anticipating his arrival.

Hours passed and Judas still wasn't home. I thought that

maybe I should call and make sure nothing happened to him on his way home. I did that several times, but he never answered. Then I began to get worried. He told me when I was there that he was finished and would be home after he cleaned up. So, by now he should be home.

Another hour went by, and I decided to call him again; the phone went straight to voicemail. *Wait a minute, now.* My next thought was *go back to that house and see if he is still there.* So that's what I did. I got out of bed, got dressed and went back to the house where I dropped the shop vac off. There was no sign of Judas anywhere. His truck was gone or at least not in front of the house anymore, and all the lights were out inside the home, so I figured the homeowner was asleep since it was so late, and he just finished working.

That only made me more worried and irritated by the minute. As I was driving back home, I was looking to make sure his truck was not at the side of the road or something; I was really just looking for any possible sign of him. His phone continued to go to voicemail. I left several messages, but nothing. By the time I got home, I was convinced that Judas was on bullshit. I was also exhausted; I needed to escape the craziness. I knew I had to get some sleep because work in the morning always comes early. I woke up at 5:30 to get ready when I realized that Judas never came home that night. I grabbed my phone, and he picked up on my fourth attempt.

"Where are you, Judas?" I asked.

"I'll be home in a lil while," he whispered.

Heartbroken, I hung up the phone and got ready for my workday.

I carried on as if nothing had happened, yet all day it weighed heavy on my mind. It was hard to push away the feeling of betrayal. I tried to rush the day at work, all while anticipating getting home as fast as I could.

Judas was there, acting like nothing was wrong. I didn't beat around the bush, I got straight to the point. "Where were you?"

He tried to tell me that he was at his parents' house because he needed some time to think. He said he had a lot on his mind, and he needed to clear his head.

I did not believe one bit of that mess of a story. First of all, Judas is a very private person, and he doesn't like people in his business. Second, Judas' world revolved around our house, and our office room was his sanctuary. If something was on his mind, he always went there to think. Now, if that was the case, why not just call me and say that? Why tell me you will be home shortly and never show? That's bullshit!

Weeks went by and Judas and I were not connecting. I was starting to add up all the changes that I saw taking place in him. As weeks passed, we talked less, and the vibe between us completely changed. More and more, I would see a different Judas evolving. This confused me because a few years prior, the two of us were solid. At least he had me believing we were. I couldn't quite figure out what was going on with him.

Sadly, it didn't stop there. There was this. Two night later, Judas came home from his part-time security job and greeted me with a kiss. He then headed straight to the shower. Fifteen minutes later, he was dressed and looking quite good, as he knows how to do, and I assumed he was going out somewhere. So, I asked him.

"I'm going over to my buddy's mother's house. He's in town and all the fellas are meeting to go have drinks." Well, if you have been reading this book from the beginning, you know that Judas doesn't just go out for drinks. Besides, he worked both jobs that night. This was totally out of character for him.

Now my patience was running short, and I was sick of all the lies. I straight up asked my husband, "Are you in these streets? Are you seeing somebody? If you are, tell me now so we can end this right here." He probably wasn't expecting me to be so forthright like that, but I had to.

Judas was defensive and said he wasn't seeing anyone. It was legit to just go hanging out with his buddies; and with those words, he was out the door. I knew at that moment that he was going to see a woman. I tossed and turned for hours and after multiple calls and a shitload of lies, he finally made it back home. By then, I was disgusted and didn't even want to see his face.

Nonetheless, I had to, because we briefly discussed his new normal of hanging out and being away from home. He tried to assure me that he wasn't doing anything wrong and there was no other woman, but a woman knows what a woman knows. I pushed through day after day, remaining watchful. Something was definitely going on and there was only one person I could depend on to guide me.

As days and weeks passed and time ticked on, Judas and I were getting into our old rhythm. We still enjoyed one another, went on dates, socialized, and maintained a safe and comfortable home front for our family. For the most part, things were good. Trust was an issue, but we were working through it. It was life as usual for a while, until I began to notice those same behaviors as before. He would wait until I went to bed at night to go downstairs to cut his hair for HOURS. Well, some may think that was a good thing because he didn't want to disturb me. Unfortunately, that was not the case.

Each day seemed to get harder and harder, knowing that

Judas was "in these streets." He would never admit it, but I knew my gut wasn't lying to me. So, one Friday morning, I woke up and out of bed, then got on my knees and I began to pray. I prayed for many things, but there was one prayer in particular I submitted before GOD. I said, "Father, if my husband is seeing another woman LORD, show her to me." As I closed out my prayer and rose from my knees, the weight that seemed to be pulling on me was lifted. I felt better instantly, and I really didn't know why.

The weekend passed and Monday morning came fast enough. Judas and I were both up, getting ready for work. The Nissan Armada we had was in the shop for repairs, so Judas was driving a loaner car. Whenever we need to get a loaner car, the dealership always gives us the newer version of what we already have. Well, we know that's their tactic to get us to upgrade and spend that money. We were in love with our Armada, so we weren't looking to upgrade at the time.

Judas had the car for a couple of days before I had the chance to check it out. Any time he had to get a loaner car he would always tell me, "Baby come check out this car." For some reason, this time he didn't do that, and I didn't think much about it either. However, while he was getting ready for work one Monday morning, he said, "Baby, you didn't see the car yet."

"Oh yeah, let me go see it right quick." I grabbed the keys and went into the garage.

I walked around the car a couple of times to check out the exterior and it was pristine. Perfect. Then I got inside to see all the features. I played with the buttons, opened compartments, and started the engine to see how quiet it ran. That's what people do when their new toy (for the time being) is a brand-new car. No big deal, but there in the middle compartment was a cell phone that I knew wasn't Judas', so I figured maybe the last person who had the car or one of the salesmen left his phone there. *Oh well,* I thought.

As I stepped one foot out of the car, I paused long enough to reach around and grab that phone. It was a spontaneous move on my part. The message, "look at the phone" flashed across my brain. That flash of a moment revealed a photo of a woman on the screensaver. Right away, I recognized the picture. I had seen it before.

Six months prior to this new revelation, one of Judas' Metro Police buddies texted him that picture. How do I know? I was laying across the bed with him when it came to his phone. I did not inquire about the picture at that time because I knew Judas and some of his officer friends shared naked pictures of women from time to time. I thought this was just another "eye candy" photo.

Recognizing that picture was enough to decide to look further, so I found myself scrolling through my husband's secret phone. Something we both never did to the other. My heart was going 1000 beats per minute, and I was running out of time; I was afraid I would get caught. I should have been heading back to the house, but I just couldn't put down the phone. There were multiple text conversations with several women who I knew, some of whom claimed to be "family friends" and had been in our home and eating at the dinner table with our family as 'friends'. There were erotic pictures and pictures that were clearly taken during a sex encounter with one of the women. There were pictures of the woman on the screensaver with the white Maltese dog that I asked Judas to buy me for Christmas. No, he didn't buy me the dog. He said we didn't need another dog because we already had one (Kimora).

Let me tell you, I was reading those texts so fast my head was spinning.

I was only in the car for a short time, but it seemed like forever. With all the stuff I saw on that phone, I was DEVASTATED. Nevertheless, reading wasn't enough. Judas was seeing three women from the text messages regularly. He reached out to his ex-wife prior to me, but she didn't respond.

I learned that he was seeing three different women on a consistent basis. He texted the same exact message to each

THE COST OF DISOBEDIENCE

woman separately, as if he was reading from a script. All three women with different text threads but the same exact messages. Of the three, one stood out. The one whose picture was on the screensaver.

Knowing that I was running out of time, I got out of the car, closed the door, and went back into the house, with his private phone still in my possession. Trying to compose myself with my anxiety out of control, I turned to Judas and said, "The car is nice. Well, okay. Gotta go before I am late for work."

I kissed him like I have done when either of us leaves the house, and out the front door I went. With the phone in my pocket, I clenched the steering wheel with all my might as I slowly drove away from the house. I didn't want to be late for work, and I was shaking like a leaf. Clearly, Judas had forgotten he left this phone in that compartment on the armrest.

Once I drove a few blocks away and was out of view of the house, I stopped on the side of the street to pull myself together. My mind was racing, and I was hysterical. I had never cried like this before. What I had been thinking all along was true. My husband is having an affair. What's worse, it's not just with one woman, it's multiple women. Who does this? And how come I didn't see it?

At that point, going to work was out of the question, and

once I surrendered to that thought, I drove to the nearest parking lot and settled in a spot to park so I could continue searching Judas' phone. It did not take me long to decide that I needed to call the woman in the pictures. I wanted to find out why she was on the screen in the first place.

The phone rang once, and she picked it up. "Good morning, Mr. Isharat" was whispered in a soft and sexy kind of way.

I responded quickly. "This is not Mr. Isharat, this is Mrs. Isharat."

Nothing from the other end of the phone. I told her that I didn't know what part she played in Judas' life, but she could not have my husband and her best bet was to stay away from him. She tried to tell me she wasn't seeing him, and they were just friends.

So, I reminded her of the text messages I read. "I think you are definitely playing the role of more than just friends."

She went on to say that she would never date a police officer because her ex-husband was a Sergeant, and he was horrible. Yeah, okay! This woman was texting Judas to say she was so in love with him that it was becoming obsessive. She told him she was tired of waiting and couldn't wait for the two of them to finally be together. I ended my conversation with her by saying,

"Sorry you were the Devil's advocate, but you will never have my husband."

I hung up and called the next woman. In this case, it was a little girl. Same scenario, the sexy good morning voice, and she got the same, "This not Mr. Isharat, this is Mrs. Isharat." She burst out in laughter. I offered her the same opportunity to stay away from Judas.

All she could do was laugh at the situation and me. "She said, "As long as he keep running that dick over here, Imma keep fucking him." I knew then this was clearly a young girl with her head screwed on backwards. There was no need to continue talking to her. I left my conversation with her with a warning. If I ever caught her with Judas, it would be tragic.

By this time, Judas was in the loaner car and calling me back-to-back. I knew he was on to me. He realized the phone was missing. Reluctantly, but at the same time wounded and angry, I answered. "Hello!" Judas said. "Why the fuck are you going through my phone calling my friends?"

Wait. What? Did this ninja just call and question me about the side pieces he messed with? Indeed. Yes, he did. I went back and forth with him for about five minutes over the phone before we ended the argument with him controlling his anger and probably gritting his teeth. He then said: "Bring me my damn phone and bring it now".

I hung up and called my friend Lasagna and told her everything that had just happened. I told her I couldn't take it anymore and I was leaving Judas.

I'm glad I called her because she comforted me and gave me her thoughts about the situation and about Judas.

I headed back home, praying all the way that Judas would be there, but he wasn't. He went on to work. By the time he came home that evening, everything about me was lit up and I was in full force.

We discussed the phone and all the pictures and texts I found. He never denied any of it and his only defense to me were these words: "I love my wife. I ain't going nowhere." I wish I was making this stuff up, but I'm not. This man was crazy. Well okay, let's see if Ms. Smitty knows the same.

While Judas was claiming his love for me, what he did not know is I had the lady on the screensaver on the house phone. So, while he was saying she meant nothing to him and that he loved me and would never leave me, she heard it all. I'm not sure what happened on her end of the phone, but Judas heard something come from the phone receiver. He grabbed the phone and when he realized it was connected to Ms. Smith's phone, he threw it across the room. It smashed into the wall and broke.

That's when Judas raged out the back door. Before he left, he turned to look at me and spewed his ugly words. "You ain't shit, you dirty bitch!" Now, I chuckled at that because the ball was now in my court. All this time Judas had been running around town like a single man. Ms. Smitty told me that Judas remodeled her house, bought her kids the dog for a Christmas gift and told her that he had been trying to divorce me for years. Judas allegedly told her about the whole incident with Babygirl in 2009 and that he should have left me then. Well, Ms. Smitty should know that you can't trust liars and cheaters, so what she was saying was probably 50% BS. She lied about who hooked her up with Judas. (I knew who hooked them up, and she wasn't being honest but that's beside the point.)

I left our home for a while and stayed with my oldest daughter until Judas finally tracked me down and persuaded me to go back home. There was no doubt about it. I loved my husband very much. I never wanted to be without him, but his behavior was beginning to be a bit much. There were several times where I reached out to his sister to say, "Hey, if your brother doesn't get his shit together, I'm going to leave him!" I would give her grave details of some of the things he was doing to me. Each time she would say, "Wait Sis, don't leave him, let me talk to him." So, I didn't leave him. I hoped she would talk some sense into him, but clearly, that did not happen.

After the flood of tears, phone calls, and amazing gifts, I went back home to Judas. Sad but true. Hell, I love my husband. For a few months, things were good, but then things only got worse. That's because I was no longer sitting by and being a door mat. I was no longer allowing shit to go unaddressed. I was no longer allowing my husband to handle or talk to me in any unkind or aggressive way. If something was wrong or inappropriate, I addressed it and did so with authority. In an attempt to re-focus myself and redirect my thoughts, I enrolled in a nursing program to advance myself in my career. I guess you can say it was a way of escape for me.

While I still loved Judas, still treated him like a king, and still respected him as my husband, it wasn't enough to change his behavior. It seemed it made it worse. With all the hell I've been through with him, the more I forgave him, the more f*cked up things he did. You would think that because I left, and he begged me to come back, he would be on the straight and narrow when I came home. NOPE! It got worse. How much worse can it get after an affair?

One day I got a call from Judas, but because I was working, I couldn't answer it, and the message went to my voicemail. When I got a chance to listen to it, I saw he called and so I played the voicemail. Clearly, the voicemail was not meant for me. It was a

THE COST OF DISOBEDIENCE

voicemail from Judas at work telling a female coworker how he wanted to explore the piercing that she disclosed that was in a "private" place on her body. I replayed and listened to the voicemail several times to be sure I heard what I thought I heard. When I got home from work, I asked him about it.

As he sat at the end of the bed and began to take off his work shoes I said to him, "sorry I missed your call, I was busy at work today". He replied by saying, "no worries it's all good". At this point I'm wondering did he call me on purpose and forget to hand up or did his phone "pocket dial" me? I then went on to say, "so you want to see someone's piercing at work"? Immediately becoming defensive, he responded, "What"? I repeated my question, "who's piercing do you want to see at work"? And I began to play the voicemail on speaker phone so he could hear it.

Immediately he apologized and tried to make me believe that this is how "they play around "at work in the locker room. My next question after that was,"so the men and women share locker rooms"? He never responded to that question, and I really didn't give him a chance as I began to remind him of all the bullshit and pain that he has put me through. Again, he apologized and said he wasn't going to do anything to lose me. Well ultimately, that was a lie. I didn't waste my time to argue with Judas, I had studying to do for school.

It was only three months later before Judas strikes again. Judas wasn't home but left his iPad out on the dresser. Usually it's locked away, or turned off and require a password to unlock, but that day it wasn't. He clearly had to forget it was unsecured. I was watching TV and heard the iPad notifications go off, so I touched the home button, and the screen came on. Lo and behold what was before my eyes. His first wife sending pictures of herself in lingerie with the message telling Judas to "Like Nike Just Do It." Now of all the other shit I have seen, this floored me. Again, another person who has been in our house proclaiming to be "family." Someone whose house I've been to many times and shared good times with.

From the very beginning of our courtship, Judas always swore to the fact that he and his first wife were ONLY friends and had a great co-parenting relationship. I had no reason to doubt him and I'm all for healthy co-parenting. Again, Judas would take me to her house to visit his kids and we would socialize and have a good time.

When Judas's second graduated from the police academy, maybe about a year prior to the iPad notifications, I suggested that we have this huge party for him at our house. First Judas said no, but I was able to change his mind. Begrudgingly, he said, "Okay, but his momma can't come." At the time, I didn't understand why he was so adamant about her not coming. I was all for her being there because it was a big accomplishment for their son. Putting two and two together, I may have reunited the relationship then between her and Judas. While Judas was acting like he didn't want his kids' mother in the house for the celebration and her staying secluded to herself all night claiming she was "watching" the grandbaby makes me now think something was going on between them all along. Was it guilt that made him not want her there? Was it guilt that kept her secluded in that room saying she was watching the baby?

So, the voicemail, the iPad pictures, when does it stop? All this mess is now becoming a distraction to me and it's affecting my grades at school.

Well, it never did. More often than not, we argued. Then he began insisting that I not go to places without him. He kept my phone line tied up for eight hours while I was at work so no one else could get a call through. On one occasion, he had AT&T interrupt my line so I couldn't call anyone. He did that because he had gotten into an argument with me. Judas had become very controlling, insecure, and aggressive over the years, but it hadn't really manifested until I stopped taking his shit.

I knew our marriage would be over soon because Judas had started doing the one thing, I said I would NEVER tolerate: ABUSE!

Now listen, I'm not saying I'm an angel. I can be hell on wheels when my fuses get blown. I'm not the one who's going to sit back and be disrespected and just let someone run over me. The first time, you may get a pass, the second time you will get a warning. The third and final time all hell will break loose. Like Tupac said, "I ain't no killer, but don't push me".

Our arguments had become toxic. As a matter of fact, the entire relationship had become toxic. When Judas would get angry, he would call me degrading names in front of my teenage son. We argued a lot, but it seemed like when he had an audience, he really went at it. It didn't matter if there were cousins, friends, my kids, his kids, in town or out of town, boy, if he had an audience, he was going to show his ass. The disrespectful things he would say in front of my son was unimaginable and heartbreaking.

The vulgar disrespect then led to him eventually physically fighting me. One time he tried to punch me in the face while he was driving us home from Aunt Jazzy's house after we had funeralized her brother. On a different occasion, he choked me because I stood my ground and attended a women's retreat with some friends in Buffalo, Michigan; it was something he didn't want me to go to. Many times, he would put his feet on me and kick me out of the bed if I didn't have sex with him. The straw that broke the camel's back was when Judas attempted to fight with me, and my son and his classmate were in the basement of our home. Ya'll this man was CRAZY!

Judas was in a rage again because he had become so insecure and controlling, and when things were no longer going his way, he couldn't handle it. As we were arguing in the house, he started saying very inappropriate and disrespectful things and the boys could hear him.

I headed toward the door, telling Judas, "I'm not about to do this with you."

I looked up and there he was, blocking me. I went back into the bedroom as we continued to argue. Next thing I knew, he grabbed the can of Pepsi on the nightstand and flung it at me with a force I had never witnessed. The can made contact and cut my left arm. Before I knew it, I jumped across the bed and was fiercely beating and punching his face. Once I realized what I was doing, I backed away. Judas' face was bleeding from his nose and my arm was bleeding because the can he threw sliced my skin.

Apparently, Judas was taken by surprise when I started hitting him, because he balled up on the bed and kept taking the punches. The minute I turned away, he yelled, "I'm calling the police! I'm calling the police! "You are a maniac"!

The minute that can sliced my arm, I didn't give a f*ck about his police threat. "Call the police," I answered. "I will be right here waiting for them." He knew better than to call the police, but he roused the interest of my son and his friend, who heard the entire commotion, and were laughing at Judas laying there on the bed, screaming about calling the police. Both those boys were also ready to do what sons do when someone is trying to hurt their mom. I assured my son that I was okay and that I would handle it. Reluctantly, he followed my wishes and the commotion ended. I cleaned myself up and migrated downstairs for the night.

No form of abuse is ever okay. Whether it be mental, verbal, or physical. It's never okay. There is no excuse for it. Period. It was time for me to leave this marriage. I had put up with enough. My mind was made up. Not to mention, all this mess has caused me to fail my nursing rotation which now pushes me back a whole year before I can pick back up and move forward in the program. I AM DEVASTATED!!! I simply deserved better. Better for me and better for my son who was still living at home with us. At this point, I just need to come up with a plan.

I tried everything to keep myself sane when I found out about the affairs Judas was having, through the lies, the behaviors, everything. My thoughts were overwhelming; and I never found peace. I felt trapped inside my own thoughts; I figured, the sooner our marriage was dissolved, the sooner I could get on with my life. But when and how will I do that? Only

GOD knows at this point.

Once againagain, I threatened to leave Judas and he faked a heart attack and manipulated me into staying. I'm talking about straight out of a television script. He laid it on thick. He said, "the thought of losing me would kill him" and he "couldn't make it without me". So, what did I do? After days of going back and forth with myself and feeling sorry for him I stayed. But it would'nt be long. Once again, once the smoke cleared a few months down the line, Judas started tracking my car, following me, accusing me of having an affair every time he saw me talking to anyone he didn't know. It didn't matter if it was a woman or a man, in Judas' mind, I was f*cking them all. As months passed me by, life with Judas and his behaviors had become all too much for me.

Matthew 11:28-29

Come unto me, all (ye) that labour and are heavy laden, and I will give you rest.

11 THE RELEASE

Chapter 11

Happy New Year 2017!!! It's a new year and I have many things to look forward too. My New Year's prayer was for this year to be the of turnaround. Meaning all the bad and negative things in my life will turnaround for my good. We brought 2017 in with a bang. Because of our work schedule we had a very private yet peaceful New Year's Eve. The next couple of days were great also. Needless to say, with only 3 days into the New Year, Judas was back at it again.

He was mad because I posted a meme on Facebook. It wasn't negative or anything I thought he would be mad about. he real reason he was mad is because my attention was not on him, but on social media. I've just spent the last four hours in our office watching television together and the entire time he had nothing to say. As soon as I focus my attention somewhere else, the drama begins. He made it seem like he owned me.

As Judas began to carry on, I told him with full intent, "I'm not spending another year in this marriage and dealing this this B.S. **I will not.**" I suppose he thought it was another threat that I wouldn't follow through with. I could understand how he thought that, but this time it was different. I was sick and tired of being sick and tired. I had no more energy for arguments and chaos Additionally I resumed my schooling and was concerned about falling behind again because of all the chaos going on in my marriage. In school, there was a test every Monday and like clockwork, every Sunday Judas would find something to argue about.

Do you know what happened on Monday mornings? I did poorly because I spent the night arguing with Judas about stupid stuff. It soon became apparent to me that he didn't want me to succeed in this nursing program. I can go into a lot of reasons why he felt that way, but suffice it to say, his words and actions affected everything around me. I could no longer turn the cheek to all his behaviors. I wanted more, deserved more so finally I decided to stand firm and leave this marriage as I should have done a long time ago and continue to pursue my desires.

It is sad but it is true. Sometimes unknowingly, we love others more than we love ourselves. How, may you ask? By allowing someone to treat us "less than" without any consequences. We as human being, both male and female teach people how to treat us based upon what we except from them. I must stress that ABUSE of ANY KIND is NEVER ok. But I allowed it by staying and turning the other cheek in so many instances that the behaviors of my husband had become like second nature to me.

However, THANKS BE TO GOD, that he gave me a desire deep down on the inside that would be my motivation to free myself from this toxic marriage that I struggled with walking away from in previous years. So yes, it came down to this: stay in this toxic marriage and continue to build up and encourage a man who won't do the same for me or pursue my goal and finish nursing school and live a better life with whatever awaits me in the future. That was the hardest decision I ever had to make, and I knew I needed guidance. It's much easier to *say* you are leaving a person than the actual leaving. Stay with me readers, I know you are probably saying, "Huh, I would have been left him". Well until you have walked in the shoes of a person being abused on any level, you can never fully understand "why they stayed so long".

I knew leaving Judas was the best thing for me, but how do I leave someone I love? Even when it's toxic, it's hard to walk away. Some of you reading my words know exactly what I mean. Was I really ready to give up on the 11 years that I shared with this man? We had some very good times. The Judas Isharat I once knew was everything any woman would desire in a man and husband.

He was handsome, well groomed, solid career, financially intelligent, took care of the home front, solid family ties and knew how to cater to a woman. So how did we get here?

Meanwhile, I remember that day like it was yesterday. On Febuary 3rd, 2017 I was home alone, cleaning as I love to do. I began thinking about my current life situation and the possibilities of the future and what it holds in store for me next. The house was bright, and it was quiet. Weird quiet. I was mopping the living room floor when I head a small still voice say, "You are not going to finish school in this house." I froze right there in my tracks and said, "I hear you, LORD." From that day forward, the decision was no longer just a thought. It was a confirmation for me. I took that as GOD's 'way of ushering me out of something I had no business being in from the start. I knew how bad I wanted to finish school, what it meant for me to finish, and I also knew that GOD was speaking to me about over-staying in my failing marriage with a man that is trying to drag me down. That was all the confirmation I needed.

Within days of that encounter with GOD, I secured a place to live with a future move in date of Febuary 24th 2017. I bought the furniture for the house and had it held at the store until move in day. I also started the mail forwarding process. I did not tell Judas because I knew this would start an argument and I just did not have the desire or energy for another long-drawn-out night of arguing. Little did I know, Judas already knew I was leaving him. He knew everything. How did he know? I'm Glad you asked.

Judas had a voice recorder hidden in the house that recorded what was being said when he was not at home. I found it a few years ago, hidden in his sock drawer. It had recordings of his second wife on the phone with her mom when her and Judas were going through their divorce. It also had conversations recorded of times when we were in Judas truck, arguing the entire time. It was always about accusing me of having an affair. He wanted me to admit that, to say those words. The fact is, I wouldn't say those words because I never had an extramarital affair. In hindsight, he was recording these arguments, pushing me to admit that I was guilty of such a sin, when he was the one sinning. How ironic. Or better yet, maybe he was looking for a reason to leave me.

On the morning of February 17th, when Judas got out of bed, he saw me cleaning the cabinets in the kitchen upstairs. The first thing out of his mouth was: "What are you doing, gathering up what you're taking?

I looked up from the bottom cabinet, somewhat surprised, and said, "What?" He then went on about my 3-bedroom, 2-bath house with the garage, driveway, and big backyard. He let me know that he knew. When I picked my jaw up from the ground (whole time, laughing on the inside) – I just stood firm, shrugged my shoulders, and said, "Okay. Now you know."

He went on to say he heard me telling my oldest daughter all about it. It was no surprise to me that he had been recording me again, but I didn't care. I was glad, even relieved, that he knew. He asked me, "So how soon are you leaving?"

"The 24th, I replied.

He got nasty. He said, "Thank GOD! The 24th can't come quick enough!"

So, I continued cleaning up and going about my day. He accused me of taking stuff and storing up for my new place and I just laughed. I was never storing up anything from the cabinets. I was simply cleaning and organizing. When the 24th came, the only thing I took from that house were my clothes and shoes. I did not want anything we had together. I had already purchased everything new.

That week before I left, every day was a battle. One day he hated me, and I was the worst thing that happened to him; the next day I was the best damn thing that ever happened to him, and he couldn't live without me. One day he was buying me gifts and the next day he had all my shoes packed and stacked up. Truly, this man was going through something, but I wasn't going to stick around and be his test-dummy anymore. That would not be fair to me.

February 24, 2017 is a day I will never forget. That was the day I took my life back. I know that sounds like a weird thing to say, but you would have to walk in my shoes to understand. It was one of the hardest things I ever had to do. I have been the one to walk away from every relationship I have ever been in, but this was one of the HARDEST. It hurt the most; yet it healed me in ways I never dreamed possible. Now that I was out from under that roof and away from that toxic environment, I had the chance to focus on getting myself on the path to healing and rebuilding. This was something I had wanted to do for a long, long time.

Believe me when I tell you that coming home to peace and quiet, no bickering, no demands, no attitudes, just peace and tranquility is a beautiful thing. I was able to focus all my attention on school. I had three more months left and it was crunch time. In my heart of hearts, I knew that nothing would stop me from achieving my goal. It was now up to me to flourish, and I was ready.

Leaving my home and my marriage took a toll on me. Some days I didn't think I could make it without the man I loved, and other days I knew I could. There were nights that I lay in my peaceful bed and cried, thinking about how Judas might have felt after I left him. He would call a couple times a week. Sometimes I would talk to him and sometimes I wouldn't. I couldn't bear to hear him crying and professing his love for me, asking me to come home. Slowly, he was breaking me down.

I knew that the marriage was toxic. I knew that it would be a terrible idea to go back but talking to Judas made it a difficult transition. I knew I needed to stop communicating with him and stop caring about how he feels when he never cared about how I was feeling. Every time he tried to work his sorrowful story on me, it kept breaking my heart. I was falling out of love with him because I had to, not because I wanted to. It wasn't until one night my oldest daughter called to check on me as she often did after I left Judas. We talked a lot about the situation and then I blurted out, "I miss my husband, I think I'm going back."

My daughter told me to get my emotions in check and remember why I left.

She was adamant that I remember what it was like every time I returned. She stayed tough. She asked me if I was okay with being cursed at, abused, disrespected, embarrassed, controlled and treated like trash. As I cried, I knew she was right. To this day, it was her reality check that kept me on my journey to move on.

So, I stayed the course. I stayed away. Even though it was hard, I knew I needed help to stay strong. I had such powerful urges to fix everything between my husband and me, but every time I tried it backfired. I had never experienced so deep in my heart what I was feeling with this break up.

I soon realized that I was bound to my soon-to-be ex-husband through soul ties. I knew it was going to take deliverance to unbound and release me from this man. I prayed and prayed, crying out to the LORD to please deliver me from the grips of the enemy.

Soul ties are real. We must be careful and prayerful about who we let into our lives. Once you allow yourself to be connected to others who the devil can use as a vessel, it can cost you your life. When you are bound by soul ties, you will do and allow things you may never have allowed before.

Man, alone cannot break soul ties. It takes deliverance and sometimes the casting out of demons to set you free.

This is where your personal relationship with GOD comes in. In whichever way it suits you, get to know HIM for yourself. Ask Him for guidance, ask Him to lead you, show you, tell you. Be open to hear Him; and when He speaks, LISTEN. He will never steer you wrong. GOD only wants what's best for you. You must be willing to submit and wait for what He has for you, all good and perfect things.

If only I had listened to the LORD when He sent His word through my pastor back in 2006. She looked me in the eye and said, "GOD said that is not your husband." From the moment we got married, all hell broke loose. Now I know why.

I disobeyed my Father in Heaven. I married a man who GOD said was not for me. As with any parent, when you disobey, you are punished. When you disobey, there is a price to pay. So GOD allowed me to pay the price for my disobedience. He was with me through it all, yet He still let me go through it. The cost was great, but I had to suffer through it:

Betrayal, deceit, embarrassment, heartache, disrespect, abuse, division from my children, control, and manipulation. You name it, I suffered it.

However, when I called on the LORD and asked Him to give me strength and deliver me from what was bad for me, HE SET ME FREE!

Psalms 34:17

The righteous cry and the LORD heareth,

and delivereth them out of all their troubles.

Psalms 50:15

And call upon me in the day of trouble:

I will deliver thee, and thou shall glorify me.

Psalms 107:6

Then they cried unto the LORD in their trouble,

(and) He delivered them out their distresses.

As parents, it is our job to protect our children in every aspect of life. We must love, encourage, nurture and discipline them so that they may grow to be productive, successful, and loving human beings to all.

ABOUT THE AUTHOR

Born in Chicago, Illinois, at Provident Hospital, Felecia Portwood was the third eldest daughter of nine siblings. Her parents, Beverly Smith and Mark Dunbar, are smiling down from the heavens because their now-grown daughter is a published author sharing her incredible story with the world. Portwood's family values would be similar to her parents in that she now has four children of her own; two daughters and two sons, while she endeavors to be a successful and humbled mother, wife, and business owner.

Portwood's journey would lead her to attend schools in Illinois and Utah. She is the co-owner of Smoke By Da Pound LLC, a Jerk BBQ Catering company, and there are other business ventures Portwood intends to tackle when the time is right! She will take advantage of living life to its fullest and being an obedient servant of GOD.

For many of Portwood's adult years, she was broken on the inside, but every day she would wake up and show up with a smile, encouraging others amid her many storms. This further explains her passion for helping others and the plan to write her second book because she knows that by sharing her trials and victories, she will be of inspiration to others.

Some of Portwood's hobbies include bowling, vacationing, fine dining, and spending time with family and friends. She also enjoys creating lifelong memories with her husband and children. Felecia Portwood is a GOD-fearing woman whose strong, wise, giving, loyal, firm, and surrounded by those who support her. What more can you ask for?